VOICE

in the wilderness

VOICE
in the wilderness

Allan May

nh Nelson-Hall/Chicago

Library of Congress Cataloging in Publication Data

May, Allan
    Voice in the Wilderness.

    Includes index.
    1. Nature conservation—United States.
2. Wilderness areas—United States. I. Title.
ISBN 0-88229-309-5 (cloth)
ISBN 0-88229-605-1 (paper)

Copyright © 1978 by Allan May

Manufactured in the United States of America.

10 9 8 7 6 5 4 3 2 1

CONTENTS

2036244

PREFACE

This book was a long time aborning. It was conceived, I think, when I was four or five years old, when my mother took me to a forest preserve near our home in Chicago.

Her ancestors were among the first people on the American frontier. Her brother, a homesteader in Wyoming, was among the last. She was raised in a small town in southern Illinois, and spent most of her adult life in large cities. But she retained an inbred respect of and love for nature and the outdoor world that nature governs.

She taught me about the beauties and the treacheries of the forest. She told me about trees and leaves and grass and the flowing creek. She taught me about quicksand and about wildlife that could be endearing or vicious, or both. I learned that the mosquitoes which raised itchy welts on my skin also helped feed the frogs that sang in the swamp. The bees that stung an unwary little boy were also responsible for flowers that bloom in the prairie and the apples in the wild apple trees. She loved and respected it all, and she passed that love and respect on to me and, later, to my sister. There was room for humans in the outdoors she knew and loved. She understood that humans are a part of nature. Their work could be ugly, but it could also be lovely and natural. Their presence in a natural setting to her simply added one more kind of nature's creatures to nature's landscape.

She died long before the wilderness conservationists gained power. I doubt that she was aware of their drive which, in effect, denies people the unhindered use of public lands. But if she had lived, I think she might have been saddened and angered at their philosophy and their success in imposing it on the rest of the populace.

I can't say that I ever consciously set out to learn about the outdoors. The love and respect for nature that my mother gave me manifested themselves in, among other things, curiosity. I did some of the things big-city boys do, Boy Scouts briefly, YMCA, summer camp. But mostly, as I grew up, I wandered in the forest preserve and the other places where a boy was free to wander and give full rein to his imagination and curiosity.

Still, when I joined the Marine Corps during World War II, I was green enough to pile all my blankets on top of me and when I woke in the middle of the night, it took me several minutes to realize why I was so cold underneath. The Marine Corps taught me other things, too, about nature in all her moods, good and bad. But for all that, my real education and enthusiasm for outdoors came after I graduated from college and moved to Washington State, where I could see the Olympic mountains from my kitchen and the Cascades from across the street.

Cautiously, timidly at first, my family and I ventured into the foothills. As our experience increased, we hiked deeper and deeper into the forests, higher and higher into the mountains. I read a great deal. I took a few courses. I learned from hiking and backpacking companions. Fortunately, my work as a journalist put me in contact with the U. S. Forest Service and U. S. Park Service and their counterparts on the state level. I made many friends in those services and I learned a great deal about how and why they manage the land and the pressures they face.

I don't claim that I learned to be an expert in the forests and mountains. Rather, I learned that there really are no experts. The forests and the mountains are so vast, so complex that even the people who live and work there all their lives know only a little of what there is to know. And those who know the forests and mountains best are those who admit they have a great deal to learn. They have learned well about some specific part or parts. They may know well about a small piece of the geography or some specific field of knowledge such as how trees grow, or how the rock was formed or the habits of wildlife. But no one knows it all and in my experience those who claim to really know the least.

So at the outset, I must admit that I have more interest in than knowledge about the forests and mountains that I love. I have climbed some of the highest peaks in my part of the country but I consider myself a hiker, backpacker and camper rather than a climber. I love to explore new places, forests, meadows, ridges where I have never been before. I love to return to those same places to see what I missed earlier and the changes that have taken place since. I especially love to go to the places where miners, homesteaders, shepherds, old time loggers lived and worked and struggled. Often the remnants of their tools and shacks and machines still are there, still solid enough to provide a picture of what they once were, still ready to feed the imagination with the stories of the men who lived there.

For, contrary to the wilderness movement philos-

ophy, the forests and mountains are people places.
Those parts that are public lands are just that, public
lands, and except for some small areas set aside as
museums with "do not touch" signs, they should be
opened for people to love and enjoy.

That is not happening under the National Wilderness Act, at least not as it is being administered now.
One reason is that it is being administered by confused men. They are confused because they work for
government agencies largely controlled by wilderness-conservation groups that long since have lost
interest in the public, wilderness and conservation.
These public servants hear only that one voice and
they mistake it for the voice of the general public.

As the years pass, more of the back- country places
I have learned to love are either declared wilderness
or set aside to be managed as wilderness even though
Congress has not yet designated that they should be.
And with each year the bureaucracy seems to redouble its efforts to "protect" the wilderness with
wilderness-destroying rules, regulations, permits,
directions and the police officers they euphemistically call wilderness rangers. That brings constrictions and dullness to places that above all else should
be free and bright. The result is an evergrowing
atmosphere of psychic morass where spiritual
beauty should blend with nature's wonders. In such a
place the promise is lost, there can be no refuge from
the pressures of a technological world. The necessity for dealing with bureaucracy has become part of
the wilderness where people go to escape bureaucracy.

The wilderness-conservation people have built
their power on many foundations. Among the most
important is their propaganda machine that turns out
vast volumes of material declaring themselves defenders of the public's interests. Ever more public

land, they say, should be encased in their wilderness system and anyone who questions that program is put down as a minion of industry. Industry, all industry, is evil, according to their philosophy.

One book by one writer who happens to love the outdoors won't counteract the reams and volumes of propaganda the wilderness-conservationists have pumped out over the years. But it may help. It may help people to understand that the wilderness is endangered by those who say they are protecting it. Perhaps that one book can lay bare the methods that have given the wilderness-conservationists power far beyond either their numbers or their reason. Many books have been published on the wilderness. Nearly all, as far as I know, have been part of the wilderness-conservation propaganda. This one is intended to counter that propaganda. The democratic system, to work well, requires that all sides of a question be aired. This is the other side of the wilderness question.

I hope the book will be read by people who share my love of the outdoors, the growing number of people I meet in the back country who have planned and worked in anticipation only to have the hike ruined by bureaucratic rules, regulations, regimentation. The police officer-wilderness ranger has destroyed too many trips to what should be wild, free land. More and more people in the back country are beginning to publicly doubt the explanations and propaganda. I hope they will read this and become convinced, active in preventing overzealous protection of the wilderness.

If, by chance, a journalist or two happens to find something of interest about our profession in this book, so be it. If a political scientist becomes interested in my observation of how small groups can manipulate the system to their own uses, so much the better. But my fervent hope is that the book will inform and influence people who share my interest in the forests and the mountains including both those who actually tramp the trails and meadows and those who hope to someday. May it give them a better insight to wilderness as I learned about it long ago in that forest preserve.

CHAPTER ONE

This book is about the American wilderness and the wilderness movement and the wilderness organizations; what they are and what they do and the grotesque irony of wilderness being destroyed by its own protection.

The wilderness program is part of the nation's preoccupation during the 1960's and early 1970's with conservation and the environment. That preoccupation manifested itself in events such as the Earth Day observances when thousands of youngsters were dismissed from school to spend a few hours roaming roadsides picking up trash. The preoccupation resulted in the growth of "environmental" organizations, some new, some converted from different causes and others which had long been in that activity but suddenly found themselves overwhelmed with new members, new wealth and new power. The awakened awareness of environmental causes brought about new laws, new policies, new agencies designed to preserve the ecology, save the world from disaster and punish polluters.

As sometimes happens with national preoccupations, the environmental movement evolved into a kind of hysteria and while many of the new laws, new policies and new agencies were necessary and desirable, others were ludicrous and/or harmful. The hysterical era of the movement had subsided by the mid 1970's and the country began to reexamine what it had done in its earlier paroxysm.[1] Hopefully it will retain what is good and necessary and discard the unnecessary and harmful.

The reexamination is just beginning and it will take some careful work to sort out the excesses. As part of that process it might be well to look at some of the environmental episodes of the early, hysterical period. That may make it easier to understand what has happened and what must be done. As it happens, I personally was involved as an observer in two such incidents. One involved the wilderness, the other concerned the different but closely related anti-pollution movement as it was manifested during what turned out to be a rather minor oil spill.

I knew, and know, little about oil spills. But it happens that I am a reporter for the *Daily Herald* in Everett, a medium-sized industrial city on Puget Sound in Western Washington. Anacortes was part of my beat. When the first stories about an oil spill in Padilla Bay, the harbor at that city, came over the wire services, the news desk sent me out to cover it.

That's one thing you become accustomed to after you've been in the fascinating business of journalism for a while. You're expected to be an instant expert on anything that happens on your beat. In this case my beat covered the counties north of Everett. Anacortes is north of Everett so the Anacortes oil spill was mine.

It was the afternoon of April 26, 1971. One of the desk men handed me a wire story that described a "major oil spill" from a barge at the pier of a Texaco refinery in Anacortes. "Might develop into something," he said. "Maybe you'd better go take a look." So I left for Anacortes.

My Volkswagen took two hours to get me to Anacortes, a small city on Fidalgo Island in the northern part of Puget Sound. I drove to the Texaco refinery but it was late. The office was locked. I couldn't see any sign of a great catastrophe having occurred. As a matter of fact, I couldn't see much sign of anything.

I drove downtown and bought some gas. "Have you heard anything about an oil spill?" I asked the young man who cleaned my windshield.

He looked startled. "Not here," he said.

"No," I said. "Out in the bay, at the Texaco refinery."

He smiled. "This is a Shell station. We try to stick to selling it." He suggested that I go up to a scenic viewpoint on a hill high over the bay.

There was no sign of an oil slick on the water, but the scenery from the viewpoint was beautiful, with the bay in the foreground and the Cascade Mountains in the background. A ship was tied up at one of the two piers that jut into the bay from the opposite shore. I saw a lot of oil tanks and refinery equipment behind the pier and the ship looked like a tanker. I framed the scene between some trees and took a picture.

A handful of people were at the viewpoint. One couple behind the trees where I took the picture obviously didn't want to be bothered, but I asked the others if the pier where the ship was tied was the Texaco pier. None knew. None had heard about an oil spill.

One man said he had come up to look at Mount Baker, in the Cascades, because he was going to climb it that summer. Baker is, maybe, forty miles from Anacortes but easily visible from where we stood. I had climbed it a couple of years before so we talked for a while.

Then I went home, convinced that if Anacortes was the site of a major oil spill, oil spills weren't as awesome as I had heard. But I had a lot to learn about oil spills.

The next morning I fast-talked the deskclerk into using the photograph I had taken; it was not exciting but it was fairly scenic. I called the Texaco refinery to ask if there was anything new about the oil spill that I could use in the picture caption. The girl on the Texaco switchboard hesitated when I told her what I wanted. "I'll let you talk to Mr. Kiersted. He's here from California," she said.

Mr. Kiersted eventually came on. He was, he told me, J. C. "Kris" Kiersted, Texaco's West Coast manager for public relations. He had flown up from Los Angeles. "What for?" I asked.

"Well," he said, " we want to work with the media on this thing, we want to make sure that all your questions are answered and that you get the right information." He explained that, frankly, he was afraid that some exaggerated and twisted stories might be spread regarding the oil spill and his company might be hurt. "Some reporters will print information without any verification at all, just because somebody said it. We want to try to see that only factual information is disseminated," he told me.

So I asked him, "What are the facts?"

He told me that a barge belonging to the United Transportation Company had been tied to the pier I took the picture of. It was loading oil from Texaco's pipes. The barge crew inadvertently left a valve open and 200,000 gallons of light diesel oil spilled out of the barge into the bay. It was dark and the spill went undetected until someone noticed the gauges on the pier indicated more oil had been pumped onto the barge than the gauges on the barge indicated were in its tanks. The crew looked around, found the open valve, closed it, and notified the proper authorities.

"Look," I told Kiersted, "I went to Anacortes yesterday and looked at your pier. There was a ship but no barge."

"The barge finished loading and left yesterday morning."

"I didn't see any oil slick, either."

"The oil was carried out of the bay on the tide."

"So, what's the problem?"

"Well, we understand the south and east beaches of Guemes Island were washed by the oil as it went by and apparently a great deal of harm was done to the aquatic life there."

"The fish?"

"Well, yes, but more so to the beach animals and, especially, to the water fowl that might have been in the area where the oil went. Then, too, there's the possibility that the oil may do some more damage as it continues to be carried by the currents."

"How much damage has been done?"

"I don't know. We have a team of scientists flying in from places like New York, Texas, and Virginia to study the situation."

Meantime, he told me, volunteers were collecting birds from the beaches on Guemes and caring for them. Oil, he said, affected the birds' feathers and they could neither fly nor float. So they would swim to the nearest beach and try to preen their feathers clean. That would get the oil into their systems and they would get sick. Often they died.

"How many sick and dead birds are there?"

"I hear they have found about 125 so far. I don't know how many are dead but I think at least some of them are."

He gave me the phone number of the bird rescuers' headquarters. I checked some other sources and read the wire service stories and the morning papers. Then I wrote a story describing how a special team, previously organized, had responded with tugs and 1,000-foot sweeps to collect the oil. The oil slick had by then moved twenty miles west, toward the Pacific.

I gave the desk as much as I had and went to Guemes to see what I could find for the next day's paper. Guemes is a medium-sized island across the channel from Fidalgo, the island on which Anacortes is situated. They are more than a stone's throw apart, but not much more. Guemes has a few blacktopped county roads, mostly along the beaches. There are a few dwellings beside some of the roads, mostly summer places of the reasonably well-to-do.

In 1971 people got to Guemes on a little motor ferry from Anacortes. It would make the trip in something like ten minutes and carry about a dozen cars, packed tight. I don't know that it had ever had a full load before the great oil spill.

But it certainly was a crowded ferry the day after the spill. The boat had just left when I arrived at the landing pier. There were cars waiting although the ferry was only halfway across the channel. I suppose there were too many to load and the ferry left without them. It made little difference, though. Instead of tying up for a long wait as they often did, the crew simply unloaded and headed back for Anacortes. "We haven't been following the schedule since early this morning," one of the crewmen told me as I boarded. "We've been running as fast as we can and we still can't keep up." Several vehicles behind me on the pier couldn't crowd on and were left behind.

As we headed for Guemes the passengers gathered in clusters at the rail. There were about twenty-five or thirty people. They included business-and-professional persons in expensive sports clothes and driving expensive cars. At the other pole were long-haired, unwashed young people in torn, faded denim who were driving smoky, noisy, old cars. Some of their cars obviously served as both transportation and habitation.

All of these people had come together in response to announcements on the radio that volunteers were needed to help the sick and injured birds. I understand that some radio stations exaggerated and embellished the situation, claiming there were vast numbers of birds in urgent need of help.

Eavesdropping on some of the conversations gave me some insights. There was a desire to help and a sense of working together to fill a need, I think, but there was more to it than that. The middle-class people seemed to be there, at least partly, because they were curious, because saving birds was a mild adventure to break up dull days at the office or bridge club. They seemed more than a little upset that the party was open to hippies.

The denim-clad dropouts shared the other passengers' sense of adventure, I think. But they also were responding to what they perceived to be a political mission. The evil business world had committed this great crime and the dropouts were responding both to prove that their lifestyle was superior and to show the world they were willing to make sacrifices in order to right the wrongs of evildoers. They seemed more than a little upset to see some evil business types responding to the same call.

Two things, I noticed, both groups had in common.

First, they were incensed and self-righteously angry at the oil industry in general and Texaco in particular because of the oil spill. (Actually, Texaco was not responsible. The oil leaked from someone else's barge. The anger was directed at Texaco, probably, because that firm was more easily identified.) Second, without exception all had arrived in cars powered by petroleum such as the oil industry was trying to supply when the spill occurred. If any were aware of the paradox, I didn't sense it.

When the ferry landed we all drove off toward the bird savers' headquarters in a house on the opposite side of the island. The trip took only a few minutes. On the way I noticed that there were more cars and people then I had ever seen on the island. Some seemed to be wandering aimlessly.

The headquarters looked from the outside like many of the other summer places on the island, larger than a cabin, smaller than the average suburban house. It was rustically modern in design, with dark stain coloring, picture windows, and thermostatically controlled central heating.

Inside, the place was like no summer home I had ever seen. There were people everywhere—sitting, sleeping, talking, playing cards, listening to the radio, eating sandwiches. One young woman, whom I took to be the boss, was talking animatedly on the telephone. Occasionally she would pause and put her hand to her forehead in a distraught gesture and raise her eyes to the ceiling.

Downstairs, in the basement, there were more people. They were clustered around boxes and cages, each of which contained a bird or two. In some cases the people were feeding or petting the birds. In others they had the birds out of their cages and were washing them or drying them with towels. One young person (female, I think) was aiming a hairdryer at a bird in a whiskey case. I didn't count but I guess there were about thirty birds in the basement. And seven or eight people.

A young man noticed me standing near the door and approached, his face a picture of righteous wrath. "It's terrible," he said. "The dirty bastards."

"Who?" I asked.

"Texaco!" It sounded like a curse. "And there's more outside, around back."

I thanked him and headed for the door. He returned to one of the bird boxes and began to munch a sandwich. I learned later that Texaco had provided the food for the bird rescuers.

Outside there were a few more boxes of birds and a few more people. I watched for a minute but nothing was happening so I wandered away. I found a pile of dead birds, a dozen or so, I suppose. I went back upstairs in the house. The young woman was still gesturing as she talked on the phone. I waited until she hung up, identified myself, and asked what was going on.

"We've set up a field hospital here," she said. "We've got about 100 birds so far. Volunteers are searching the beaches and we expect many more soon." She also said that people in boats were searching off shore for more oiled birds.

"It's been a day and a half since the oil passed the island," I said. "How long can a bird survive on water after it's been contaminated?"

The phone rang and she answered it instead of me, managing to give me an apologetic smile and at the same time make her distraught gesture.

While I marveled, a young man edged up to me. "The oil isn't gone," he said.

"I thought it had washed through the channel."

"Propaganda," he said. "We've had a gutful of that. The island is surrounded by oil. It's on the beaches.

There are huge pools of it in the bays and harbors. It's everywhere. There will be hell to pay before it's over."

"Are there more birds?"

"Birds? Every kind of creature is being murdered out there, birds, fish, crabs, sea life, beach organisms, everything that lives in or near the water."

"They are all dying," said another young man who was sitting on the floor nearby. "Nothing can survive in that awful mess."

"Where can I see it?" I asked.

"South Beach is the worst," said the man on the floor.

"Where's that?"

"Did you come on the ferry?" asked the first man.

"Yes."

"Well, that's it. The ferry lands at South Beach."

I remembered the beach at the ferry landing, but I didn't remember seeing anything like a calamity there. Maybe I missed something. I decided to go look.

Outside the house I ran into a man I know. He had a summer place on the island and had brought his kids to see if they could help.

"How's it going?" I asked.

"Everything seems under control here," he said. "We were just going out to see if we could help find some more birds."

"I hear South Beach has been hit hard," I said. "I was going to go take a look."

"There's another place that's supposed to be even worse," he said. "It's just the other side of South Beach. Follow us and I'll show you."

We drove back to the ferry landing, turned left past South Beach, drove over a twisting ridge and down to another beach.

The beach was quiet. I had pictured its sand and

rocks being covered with a thick coat of black oil, but everything seemed perfectly normal. There were people singly and in groups wandering around the beach, apparently hunting birds. My friend sent his kids to join the hunt, while he showed me the beach. We found a couple of small pools of water with shiny surfaces that could have been oil slicks. He showed me a place where he knew beach creatures had been in the past. We pulled some little shelled things off some rocks. The yellow parts underneath receded into the shell. "They seem alive to me," I said.

"I guess so," he said. But we agreed that neither of us knew much about beach creatures. He and his kids left after a while. I left, too, but I couldn't find anything worthwhile so I returned to shoot a few more pictures. While I was looking for some more shell creatures, someone in the distance shouted, "I found one!" and began waving his arms. The people on the beach surged toward him on the run. I surged, too.

When I arrived at the scene there was a circle of people, seeming for all the world like those who stand staring at the body after a fatal accident. In the middle was a bird that seemed to me to have departed this world long before the oil had departed the barge. It hardly smelled anymore.

"We'd better take it to the first aid place," one boy said.

"Oh," said a girl, "you mean pick it up?"

"I'll get a box," someone said and ran off toward where the cars were parked. In a moment he came back with a cardboard carton and some sticks.

After some difficulty the crowd managed to balance the carcass on the sticks long enough to get it in the box. Then they picked up the box and went off toward the cars. There were about ten people. As many as could, about six I'd guess, were helping hold the box. The rest simply walked along huddled as

close as they could get without tripping the box
holders. I watched while they gently put the box in
the trunk of a car. Then they all got into their autos
and drove off in a procession headed for the "first aid
place."

I arrived back at the ferry landing just after the
ferry left. That gave me something like half an hour
to check South Beach. I lifted some rocks and fright-
ened some crabs that scurried under other rocks. I
touched some barnacles and watched them recoil
inside their shells. I pulled some other things off
rocks and watched them squirm. I looked for oil
slicks on the water or oil on the beach rocks and
found none. I'm no expert but South Beach sure didn't
look devastated to me.

I mentioned that to a fellow passenger as the ferry
pulled away. "They're all doomed," he said. "There
are a few survivors but they'll be dead within a day
or two. This beach will be barren for decades. It
always happens when there's a major oil spill. The oil
works its way down into the sand and years have to
pass before it is cleaned out. It looks fine on the
surface but underneath it's full of poison."

"How does it work its way into the sand?" I asked.
"Doesn't oil float on water?"

He looked at me kindly. "There are different kinds
of oil," he said, and walked away.

Next morning, Wednesday, I called Kiersted again.
He told me the oil slick had moved another thirty
miles west and was about halfway through the
Straits of Juan de Fuca that connect Puget Sound
with the Pacific Ocean. Texaco's team of scientists
had arrived at Anacortes and their spokesman, Dr.
M. A. Wiley, had said the oil was being dissipated
partly by evaporation but also by microorganisms in
the water. The organisms consume the oil and turn it
into harmless waste materials made up of water, car-
bon dioxide, and protein.

I called Kristi Ward, the coordinator at the bird clinic—I never was certain whether she was the woman on the phone I had talked to at the house—and learned that they had about 300 birds, 250 of them dead. I don't know if the count included the one I had seen being carried off the beach. I called some other sources, read the other papers and the wire services, and wrote a story. The desk ran it with a picture I had taken at the house of a young woman washing a bird.

That was the peak of the oil spill coverage as far as the *Herald* was concerned. The oil slick kept floating toward the Pacific and getting smaller as it evaporated and was eaten by the microorganisms. I made a few calls each day for the rest of the week but the desk people were losing interest and it was getting more and more difficult to sell them a story.

Looking back on it now, I can see that reporters for other parts of the media were having the same kind of problem. One reporter made the thing look big by writing it big. The first day, for instance, he wrote a story that generated a headline reading "Anacortes Oil Spill Perils 30,000 Geese." The story said 30,000 black brant geese, representing almost 25 percent of the entire species in the Pacific flyway, had stopped in Padilla Bay—near where the spill occurred—as they migrated north. The oil was endangering them, the story said.

I had talked to a state game man who mentioned the geese but said they had already left so I didn't use them in my story. Another paper quoted the same man as saying the bird situation "so far does not look too bad" and the first paper never mentioned the geese again. Apparently they weren't affected much.

But that paper kept the game going through the week with stories that bore messages such as "Tugs Fight Oil Spill; Bird Toll May Hit 1,000;"[2] "The shell fish along Guemes Island are dead now; the beaches will be silent with the resident grebes, loons, mergansers, and scoters destroyed;" "The basement of a vacation cabin here was the scene of both hope and tragedy yesterday as a makeshift hospital for oil soaked wild birds;" "Negligence Charged In Oil Spill;" and "Marine Life 'Wiped Out' By Spill, Ecologists Report."

Another paper, on Wednesday, ran a story saying that there were oil "rainbows" in shallow pools and oil scum that "lay like butter on the sand" of Guemes' South Beach. The reporter must have been there about the same time I was but she apparently saw things I didn't. Maybe a tide washed them away before I arrived. Or maybe she knew what to look for. She also quoted a beach resident as saying he had dug down six or seven inches in the beach sand "and it's all oil."

Another reporter on the same paper, a fine journalist whom I have admired for a long time, wrote a number of stories that simply provided facts without sensationalism. When he used inflammatory information, he presented it in proper perspective and gave the source.

I don't remember that the local television stations did much with the oil spill but some of the radio stations went pretty far out in their coverage. One disc jockey injected himself into the act by arranging for a commercial aviation company to fly some of the birds from the Guemes clinic to the sponsoring organization's base in Seattle. The birds nearly all died.

All in all, the media coverage of the oil spill ranged from fair and honest to pretty sensational. But I did not see where any reporter other than myself mentioned that the spilled oil was washing harmlessly out to sea and was being dissipated by evaporation and microorganisms. To this day some people believe the oil lay spread, inert and destructive, on the waters and beaches of the bay for days on end.

What was even more interesting, to me at least, was how the conservationists reacted. I've already mentioned how some individuals, who may or may not have been organized conservationists, gave me some inflammatory information that was less than reliable. I had been told that Guemes still was surrounded by oil long after the oil had drifted past, that everything living in or near the water was being "murdered" by the oil, that South Beach was decimated and would be barren for decades, that the oil had lodged below the beach surface, none of which was confirmed when I went to the scene to look. Conservation groups, public and private, followed to varying degrees a pattern similar to that of my informants. On Wednesday, two days after the barge crew let the oil escape, the Washington Environmental Council announced in a press release that the spill was "just a taste of the catastrophic damage that is inevitable if Puget Sound becomes a large oil port." The environmental council was conducting a highly emotional campaign to close the sound to large-scale oil transportation and the Anacortes incident was made-to-order for its emotional fire. The release said that the diesel fuel in the Anacortes spill is much more toxic than crude oil, adding, "The most toxic portions of the oil dissolve immediately and actually cannot be cleaned up.'"

The environmental council claimed that the spill was almost identical in size and composition to an earlier one in Massachusetts. That spill, the release said, was thoroughly studied and showed "massive and permanent damage to the underwater marine life of an extensive bottom area (over 5,000 acres)." The obvious implication was that the same fate awaited Puget Sound. "This oil spill was a tragic incident," the release stated unequivocally. It hinted that worse "tragedies" awaited the country if it failed to adopt the council's political program.

The Seattle Audubon Society seconded the motion
with a press release which had Mrs. Anne Mack,
president, announcing, "Shellfish along Guemes Island are dead now. Beaches will be silent this spring
with the resident grebes, mergansers, scoters and
loons destroyed." The Audubon statement brought to
mind Kiersted's complaint that "some reporters will
print information without any verification at all, just
because somebody said it."

The State Ecology Department on Thursday called
the incident "the most significant spill in the history
of the state." It followed up the next day by announcing that the spill had virtually "wiped out" aquatic
life on the tidelands of South Guemes Island and
other islands. The announcement was made after
department officials surveyed the beaches. On Fri-
day the federal Environmental Protection Agency
said it had confirmed the state officials' findings.

The statements were so strong and so unequivocal
that I began to wonder if they were talking about the
same beach I had seen Tuesday. I made a quick trip
back to Guemes to double-check. I dug into the sand
but found no subsurface oil. The crabs, barnacles,
and other beach life were still in the tidelands and
birds were there in about the same numbers as on
other beaches. The seagulls were loudly contra-
dicting the Audubon Society's statement about the
beach being "silent." I left the beach still puzzling
over the press releases. I have made several trips to
the beach since, and I am still wondering years later.

The environmental agencies must have puzzled
each other, too. The state announced that the spill
had, in addition to "wiping out" the aquatic life on
Guemes' South Beach, proved deadly on parts of
nearby Lopez and Cypress Islands. The federal
agency, however, reported no damage on those
islands. The Coast Guard made headlines by ad-

Live limpets came from rock of Guemes Island's South Beach a few days after state Department of Ecology declared aquatic life had been virtually "wiped out" by oil spill.

ministratively charging the two crewmen on the barge with negligence for letting the oil escape. The men later were exonerated.

Politicians got into the act, too. The governor, lieutenant governor, and speaker of the legislative house all made statements, and the grand old man of Washington politics, Senator Warren Magnuson, announced that he would sponsor legislation to control those who so indifferently ignore the public's needs.

Even the state's vandals got into the act. Two young people went to a Texaco office in Seattle and dumped a gallon of oil on the floor "in retaliation for the thing at Anacortes." I don't know but I imagine that, like the people on the ferry, they used gasoline to go to and from the scene.

The Department of Ecology and the Environmental Protection Agency carried the spill publicity into the late part of the year by contracting with a scientific firm in Texas to conduct a study. The Associated Press announced the study with a story from Olympia that began: "Five months and $45,000 from now, state and federal environmental experts say they hope to be able to tell what lasting effects will result from the 230,000 gallon Anacortes oil spill." A few months later, some scientists at a local college announced in advance that the Texas scientists' report would not be worth much. Perhaps the Washington scientists believed that if the government was going to spend $45,000 for a study, the money should go to Washington scientists.

But the Washington scientists were pretty much right, at that. The gist of the report, when it came out, was that the study was inconclusive and it would take another study to produce anything conclusive. That study would last five years and cost another $200,000.

The Department of Ecology people said at the time that they were studying the report and its recommendation. Several years later as I was collecting my notes on the oil spill, I called the department and asked if the second study had been approved. After some verbal sparring, the man on the phone told me the second study had not been contracted. That was about all I could get from him.

A couple of things come to mind when I think about the Anacortes oil spill: First, while oil spills are certainly undesirable and, I suspect, can cause immense environmental damage, in at least one case the damage seems to have been largely imaginary. Second, although conservationists and journalists seemed convinced that the industries involved were dishonest and their public relations spokesmen untruthful, just about everything that Kiersted told me would happen did happen, and when he didn't know something he said so. Little of the information that I heard or read from the conservationists turned out to be reliable.

Both sides were trying to sell the world on their own integrity and the morality of their cause. To me it seemed that the industry was factual while the conservationists were mostly emotional. Score one for industry.

The Anacortes spill shows pretty well that a relatively minor environmental situation can result in emotional overreaction. The news releases during the week of the spill illustrate how conservationists (individual, group and governmental) take advantage of such a situation to grab headlines and promote their causes. That the news media lent themselves to the overreaction and promotions is in part a criticism of our willingness to be misled for a good story and our tendency to rely on self-serving news sources.

If the conservationists are willing to take advantage of a ready-made opportunity to promote their causes, they also are capable of manufacturing their own opportunities. A classic example of this fact was the time Supreme Court Justice William O. Douglas came to the Cascade Mountains to save the Glacier Peak Wilderness from the Kennecott Copper Co.

The wilderness is east and north of Everett in the

far-back reaches of the Cascade Mountains. It is a half million plus acres of forest, meadow, and mountain, a rugged but beautiful place and, if you avoid the more popular spots, a lonely one.

The wilderness was created by Congress in 1964, one of the first under the Wilderness Act that became law that same year. Long before that, beginning in the late nineteenth century, miners had swarmed through the Cascades looking for gold and any other minerals that would earn them a dollar.

The first prospectors were tough, lonely mountain men who braved suffering and death in their quest, the kind of people some wilderness buffs today pretend to be. But the placer minerals that could be extracted from loose sand and gravel soon were exhausted. The less readily obtainable, rock-bound metals required large-scale capital that few tough, lonely mountain men had available. Corporations took over. They were small and local at first, then as the minerals became even more difficult to find and to mine, large and national or international.

One of the large corporations was Kennecott Copper which about the mid-twentieth century acquired some old copper claims on Miners Ridge near the center of the wilderness. Kennecott spent many years and many dollars surveying the claims and in the late 1960s let it be known that it had found the ore rich enough to make a mine feasible.

Miners Ridge is a beautiful spot on the north wall of the Suiattle River Valley, near the headwaters. It overlooks the Suiattle Valley and countless other valleys, ridges and peaks, including snowcapped Glacier Peak, the highest mountain in the wilderness.

Wilderness conservationists wanted no mines in the Cascades at all, especially on property surrounded by the wilderness. Predictably, they responded with a highly emotional campaign. They de-

clared Kennecott to be demonic and demanded that
the government stop any plans the company had for
developing a mine.

Kennecott, of course, owned the land and had spent
a great deal of money on the mineral surveys. There
was, obviously, reason for the wilderness-conservationists' opposition. There also was reason on the
other side. Characteristically, the wilderness conservationists ignored the other group's viewpoint.
They demanded that the government "save the wilderness" by enacting laws; the company's right to its
own land would simply have to be ignored.

The wilderness conservationists used all their
accustomed propaganda techniques in the campaign,
including a people's-protest demonstration.

I learned about the demonstration through a
release the news desk gave me. It is necessary, of
course, to have a fair number of people at a people's
protest. One way to get people to a demonstration is
to have a celebrity to attract them. The celebrity for
this one was William O. Douglas.[3]

The Justice was a natural choice. He was well
known. He had a high and powerful position. He had
built a reputation as an outdoorsman and as a man of
the people. The Save the Wilderness campaign was
closely associated with outdoors and the wilderness
conservationists strongly claim to be the people or, at
least, to speak for the people. Furthermore, the Justice could be depended on to espouse almost any
cause decreed by big-time wilderness conservationists.

There was a phone number on the press release, so
I called it. The man who answered told me the protest
was being sponsored by a wide assortment of wilderness conservation groups but he was the head
boss, chief organizer, and father creator. He gave me
the standard talk about evil corporations and the

brave individuals—him—who were facing them to fight for the people. The protest, he said, was only partly in opposition to Kennecott's mine. He also wanted to stop other commercial activities in the forest, including logging.

The protest demonstration, he told me, was to be held at the trail head of the Suiattle River trail. That is at the end of the road and about a twelve-mile hike to Miners Ridge. I told him I had made the hike several times so he was saved telling me how beautiful it was. The Justice was on the schedule to lead the people's protest in a symbolic hike up the trail as far as time would allow, one to five miles, probably. That would give the protesting people an opportunity to see some of the beauty that Kennecott was going to destroy.[4] At the end of the walk, the Justice would give a speech, detailing his thoughts about the mine, logging, and other such activities. They would be negative, of course.

I don't know whether the demonstrators ever knew how close they came to encountering mayhem during their demonstration. Darrington is the nearest town to the Suiattle Trail head and the mine site. The town has about one thousand people, a Forest Service district office and a lumber mill. Its only other industry is logging. The Forest Service and the mill employ a few of the men, but most others are loggers who, as they put it, "work in the woods."

There is something special about loggers. You can usually identify them by their clothing—ankle-high boots, cut-down jeans, wide suspenders, and grey, striped shirts. But even if they wore business suits they would stand out because of the width of their shoulders and the size of their biceps. Weak men do not work in the woods. The longer a strong man stays in the woods, the stronger he becomes.

The loggers' job is tough and dirty, but it is outdoors and close to nature and that provides a special

kind of experience that most people in the modern
world never know. Few loggers are highly educated
but many are highly intelligent and often they are
highly articulate. Their jobs and their towns usually
are isolated deep in the mountains and they like it
that way because they tend to be independent, self-
reliant, and somewhat suspicious of strangers.

A logger's life is dangerous and often he develops a
devil-may-care attitude. Loggers in the Cascade
Mountains possibly are the closest thing this country
has left of the wilderness pioneer. Their towns are
the closest thing we have left of the old-fashioned
frontier settlement. Loggers, generally, are the kind
of people who prefer to solve their problems themselves. If that requires violence, so be it.

A basic claim of the wilderness-conservationists is
that they speak for the people and are striving to protect the common man from the evil designs of industrialists. They have not convinced the loggers. Not
that loggers have any great love for industrialists.
Usually they do not. But in most cases they reserve a
special feeling of contempt for the kind of wilderness conservationists who would close up the woods
whether to logging or mining. The jobs that are lost
are the loggers' jobs.[5] Moreover, they resent the big
city conservationists using political muscle to re-
order loggers' lifestyles, especially since the loggers
are not consulted in the matter.

When Darrington heard that the wilderness conservationists were planning a people's-protest-demon-
stration in Darrington territory, some of the town's
more hotheaded citizens laid plans to take part. They
looked on the demonstration as an opportunity to
vent the frustrations of years of looking on, helpless
and voiceless, while the hated wilderness conservationists remorselessly destroyed the things loggers
value most.

If the loggers couldn't match the wilderness conservationists' propaganda and lobby machines, they were pretty sure they could whip them in a free-for-all fight that was even partly fair. They were probably right. Many wilderness conservationists pride themselves on their physical strength but they usually are deskbound types, and few could begin to match even the weakest loggers.

The Darrington plans for the event, I understand, grew bigger and more violent as time passed. It was not until the last few days that cooler heads in town began to realize that the situation was getting out of hand. I was not involved, of course, but friends who were tell me there was a meeting of the cooler heads a few days before the protest. Then the word went out that violence at the protest would play directly into the wilderness conservationists' hands and anyone from Darrington who took part in a disorder at the demonstration would pay Hell when he got back to town.

It worked. There was no violence at the protest. But it was a near thing and the cool heads weren't sure until it was over that their warning would be heeded.

Anyway, the day came. The loggers who showed up limited their participation to peaceful discussion. The protesters and the newsmen showed up and the protest took place.

There is a parking lot and campground near where the road ends at the bottom of the trail. I drove in and parked next to a car that was as old as my Volkswagen but a lot bigger. All four doors were opened and people poured out of all of them. There must have been a dozen, ranging from small children to young adults. They all were in ragged, faded, and dirty clothing. They were—men, women and children—using the kind of language I would have learned in the Marine Corps if I hadn't already known it. They were pretty obviously the hippie conservationists that are accepted by but sometimes embarrassing to their middle-class associates.

The driver was a nice-looking, short man who seemed friendly. I was wearing a green jacket I had bought the night before. It was zipped all the way up. He smiled and I smiled back. We chatted for a moment while I took off the jacket and put it in the car. The driver scowled a little and abruptly walked away. I figured I must have looked like a kindred soul with the jacket on, but when I took it off my clean, wash-and-wear shirt exposed me as an 8-to-5, middle-class type and he no longer approved of me. Too bad. I might have enjoyed talking to him.

I arrived earlier than most of the protesters, most of the reporters, and the Justice. Somebody told me the Justice had been delayed at a meeting and would be several hours late. There wasn't much going on yet. Most of the protesters were keeping their signs hidden until more reporters—and photographers—showed up. Some of the few signs that were on display claimed the bearer was saving the people's property. The others insulted industry, in this case Kennecott. At the request of some photographers, four or five sign bearers lined up and marched purposefully a few yards. But when the photographers lost interest, the protesters put their signs away and relaxed.

All in all, it was a scene of something waiting to happen. The wilderness conservationists were in gaggles holding private conversations and studiously ignoring the few loggers who were milling about in their logger outfits.

I wandered about looking for a story. I was beginning to think there might not be too much to write about. Eventually I found two young loggers talking earnestly to another young man, obviously a college student responding to the wilderness conservation groups' call to arms.

The student seemed a highly refined, sophisticated, intelligent, educated, concerned young man who had been saturated with the wilderness conservationists' propaganda line. He was arguing earnestly about the "destruction" of the forests, a favorite scare tactic of the wilderness conservationists. He wore the air of a missionary, sincerely and honestly convinced that he had knowledge that could serve not only the forest destroyers but all mankind if he could only make the loggers understand.

The logger who was doing most of the talking obviously had much less formal education than his adversary but was his equal in intelligence. He had the distinct advantage because they were talking about the forest which was both his livelihood and his life. I think the college man's first surprise came when it suddenly dawned on him that the logger was not just a mindless cutter of trees but a man who so loved and respected nature that he had chosen working in the forest as a career.

The college man's second surprise came when he realized that the logger, despite his lack of schooling, had a great deal of knowledge about the forest, both practical and theoretical. "Ecology" had recently become a byword among city-bred conservationists and the young man had come to spread the gospel among the heathens. Gradually the heathen was disintegrating the missionary's simplistic gospel.

"You destroy the forests," the college man said.

"This forest is overmature, the trees are dying of disease and insects. If we don't cut them, fire will get into the dry wood and the forest will go anyway."

"Soon the forests will be all gone."

"Forests regrow."

"You're cutting them faster than they grow."

"This is Forest Service land. There's a sustained-yield program. We can't cut more than grows."

It went like that for several minutes. Gradually the college man's righteous indignation turned to confusion. Finally, he tried a last sally: "You're destroying the wildlife's habitat. I saw a deer on the road on the way up here. What will happen to the deer if the forest is cut?"

"Deer don't live in dense forest. There's no browse for them. They stay in meadows and clearcuts where there is browse."

The young logger's frustrations and fears were being released. His way of life was threatened by people he considered ignorant of the issues involved. This probably was the first time he had been able to meet one of his enemies in face-to-face discussion. He was plainly overwhelmed with the emotion. He stood stiff, leaned toward the other man, his face a portrait of intensity, and nearly exploded:

"You didn't know that, did you?"

The college man didn't answer. He stood staring in front of him for a moment, his head turned slightly down, obviously disturbed. Then he walked away without saying a word.

A few minutes later a car left the parking lot. It was too far for me to see who was in it, but I like to think it was the college man going home to do some heavy thinking about simple solutions for complex problems. I didn't see him at the protest demonstration again.

Score one for the uneducated logger over the sophisticated college man.

There was more aimless waiting. A lot of it. I wandered into the woods a little way to enjoy them while I waited. I got back to the demonstration just as the Justice and his wife arrived. He was more than I expected. At first glance he seemed to be just an old man, rich and powerful enough to have a young and attractive wife. But there was more to it than that.

Just by being there he changed the complexion of the meeting. Somehow, what had been a disorganized, aimless gathering suddenly became cohesive and purposeful just because he stepped out of a car. The people who had been spread in unconnected small bunches throughout the campground suddenly, without a signal, gathered around the couple and waited for him to do his will. I am not always impressed with the breadth of the Justice's perception but for sheer power of personality I've never seen his match.

The hike up the trail was a bust. He was supposed to go one to five miles up the Suiattle, but actually all he did was walk up the last few hundred feet of road to where the trail begins. I watched. He hardly set foot on the trail.

About the only thing worth mentioning was that, as I was walking along the road, I noticed the guy who had been driving the car I had parked next to. He was walking with some of the people who had been with him in the car. He was wearing a jacket like my new one. It made him seem different somehow, because it was clean and new. I suppose it made him seem more what my grandmother would have called respectable, but he probably would refer to as square. He noticed me looking at him and appeared rather quizzical. I figured he was trying to place me so I smiled, but he had already looked away and was walking down the road.

The speech actually didn't have much more meaning than the hike. The Justice made a blanket statement that it is wrong for man to destroy nature's rocks and trees and change them to dollars. He expounded at some length on the theme. I stopped taking notes.

The young logger who had been in the discussion with the college man was standing nearby. I winked and he came closer.

"He's wrong about that," the logger said.

"About what?"

"About changing rocks and trees into dollars."

"How do you mean?"

"You don't change them into dollars. You change trees into houses and paper. Rocks you change into things like cars and airplanes and you get your dollars from the people who use those things. I noticed the Justice drove up here in a car and I bet when he came out here from Washington he flew in an airplane. Where would he be if we hadn't taken those rocks from nature?"

He sounded bitter. The frustrations that had been released in his talk with the college man were back. "Why don't you tell him?" I asked.

"I've been trying to talk to him. There are fifty people around him wherever he goes. All you can do is say hello. I don't think he'd pay any heed anyway. He's a pretty big man."

The Justice rambled on with his simplistic picture of evil corporations raping the land at the expense of the common people.

For whatever it's worth, score another one for the logger.

The thing broke up and I went back to my car. The car I had parked next to was gone. I packed my stuff in the Volkswagen. It took me some minutes to realize that my jacket was not on the seat where I had left it. I looked on the floor, beneath the seats, and under the hood. Nowhere.

It was an educational day. I learned that loggers sometimes have more insight than sophisticated college kids or famous, influential Supreme Court judges, and that you should watch your hat and coat, even in the forest.

Final score, one for industry, two for loggers, and one for guys who don't like middle-class reporters who drive Volkswagens.

CHAPTER TWO

America's wilderness conservation pressure groups have done a great deal to benefit the country in particular and mankind in general. They also do a great deal of harm—to their own cause as much as to anything else.

The harm is a result of the pressure groups' excesses, exaggerations, and distortions, coupled with the fact that they have acquired power far out of proportion to their numbers. In large measure both the contortions and the power are the result of the pressure groups having become highly organized, enormously strong, and vigorously disciplined.

Political pressure organizations, of course, are not unique to the wilderness conservation movement. Such organizations have all sorts of goals and they exist on all levels of government. They range from large, well-financed, congressional lobbies to the small and crude—but just as effective—groups that sway the thinking of the decision-making bodies in even the smallest communities.

I have no idea how many pressure groups I have watched operate in a quarter of a century of covering the news in local governmental agencies, but there have been many. A few stick in my mind. I remember, for instance, interviewing a woman who was attempting to force the school board to run the schools at her dictation. She had zeroed in on the school superintendent as her main adversary. Her complaints against him were legion. He had, she told me, hired incompetent teachers, allowed the school board to approve a school calendar that did not permit children properly to observe some holidays, purchased a school site that she did not approve of, purchased school books that she considered immoral and un-American, allowed a tattered flag to be flown at a school, and failed to cut costs even though she and some of her supporters had attended a school board meeting to protest the district's tax rate. She was especially critical of the purchase of the school site. She was aware that it had been chosen by a committee of citizens and approved by a county school site committee, but she had no confidence in their abilities. The site was wrong and no building could be built on it, she assured me. Furthermore, the most plausible explanation for its purchase was that the superintendent had accepted a bribe. "We are currently investigating that possibility," she told me in a confidential tone. If she did investigate, nothing ever came of it. The site now has a school building on it that seems suitable in every way.

She told me that her major objective was to get rid of the superintendent through resignation if possible, by discharge if necessary.

"How is your campaign going?" I asked.

"Pretty well," she said. "We've been hounding him at every school board meeting, by going to his office, and by phoning him at home. He's beginning to feel the pressure. You can tell by the way he looks and acts that it's getting to him. I'm not sure we can get him to resign but I think we'll be able to destroy his health."

Then there was the little man who became convinced that he, not the elected city council, represented the people of a city where I once worked. He attended nearly every council meeting for a year or more, making demands in the name of "the people." Often, he came alone. Sometimes he would find a cause that interested a few people and he would have a handful of followers. A few times he found highly popular causes and nearly filled the council chambers. He never came close to having 1 percent of the people of the city behind him on any cause, but he made so much noise that on at least some occasions he caused the council to act against its best judgment. All in the name of democracy. His number one enemy was a next-door neighbor who was on the council. There was a vacant street right-of-way between the houses. It had never been used as a street and there were no plans ever to use it. It was in grass and looked like a lawn. Nevertheless, the little guy and another neighbor complained that the small fence the councilman had put around his flower garden encroached on city property. The city surveyed the right of way at considerable expense to the taxpayers. One Saturday afternoon while the survey was underway, the councilman moved his fence a few inches to where the surveyor said it belonged. The survey, however, also showed that the little guy's driveway was on the street right-of-way and the other neighbor had built an extension of his house several feet into the city property. The councilman must have been terribly tempted to exert his citizen's right to demand that his neighbors vacate the city land. But he never did.

Pressure groups often declare themselves to be speaking in the name of the people. Invariably they claim to have the interests of the general public at heart and invariably they present their demands in uncompromising tones, convinced that they are endowed with absolute truth. Sometimes that conviction gets them into trouble.

There was the pressure group, for instance, that had set out to reorganize a school district's educational program. Their complaints were innumerable. The teachers, they said, were either inept or poorly led. The textbooks were poorly chosen. The educational program was poorly organized. But most of all, they proclaimed, the subjects taught were wrong. They were disturbed that the schools offered more liberal arts education than the pressure group leaders wanted, and less science and math courses than they thought necessary.

There were three or four leaders and a handful of followers in a district which probably had a population of about 30,000. They approached the school board and demanded that the district be changed to their liking. The school board demurred. The pressure group leaders announced they would throw out the school board and put people in office who would run the district properly. They called a mass public meeting during which they proposed to explain what was wrong with the district and make arrangements to right the wrongs.

They were controversial, so they got a great deal of publicity, and several hundred people showed up for the mass meeting. The leaders explained that their omnipotence was due to their immense intelligence and college educations. They had, they said, researched the subject exhaustively, and there was no room for reasonable people to doubt either their position or their plan.

The plan was, they said, to elect their own people to the school board. For that purpose, they had organized themselves into a screening committee that would investigate potential candidates and approve those they deemed qualified to serve on the board. They distributed application blanks and asked those who desired to run to fill them out and submit them by the end of the meeting. Time was of the essence, they said, because the election was only a few months away and it would be necessary to work quickly to choose acceptable candidates and organize the campaign that would put the candidates in office. They apologized for the rush but, they said, it would be two years before the succeeding election and the damage to the children in that time made it imperative that the new board be elected a few months hence.

At that moment a member of the school board who had been sitting quietly in the rear of the room rose and asked if the leaders hadn't said they had researched the situation exhaustively and assured the audience that there was no possibility of error.

They had researched the entire situation and there was no error, the chairman said. Then, asked the school board member, how did it happen they did not know that the election would take place not in a few months but a full year after that? There was a long silence while the leaders conferred in a corner of the stage. Then they announced, "We certainly will research that which was just said."

But the audience already was leaving the room.

Then there was the time a school board rented a school auditorium to a church group that refuses to salute the flag or serve in the armed forces. A local

patriotic group saw that as proof that the school
board in general and the member who made the
motion in particular were unpatriotic. They conducted a campaign to get the board out of office. It
was my beat but for the most part I ignored the
situation.

One of the patriots came to the office one afternoon and took me out for a cup of coffee. The gist of
the conversation was that the board member who
had made the motion was known to be un-American
and was not fit to live in the community, let alone sit
on the school board. The patriot felt I should take
that into consideration the next time I wrote a story
about the board.

But I didn't. I happened to know that the school
board member, during World War II, lied about his
age to enlist in the Marine Corps. He was a veteran of
the Battle of Iwo Jima. The patriot who was com-
plaining not only had managed to avoid service
during the war but had become more than moderately
wealthy by dealing in the black market on a whole-
sale basis. Somehow, I felt there was confusion on
the criteria of patriotism.

Pressure groups number only a small portion of the
population, but, well operated, they can be effective
despite their small numbers. In some cases a single
person can exert tremendous pressure provided he
has access to the media and other instruments of
power. A newspaper reporter I know had an interest
in some land a school district wanted for a new
school building. He refused to sell and the district
threatened to condemn the land. There was no other
suitable property in the vicinity where the school
was needed. The site had been recommended by the
engineer, the architect, the county planning commission, and a school site committee. Everyone was in
favor of it but the reporter.

He conducted a campaign that consisted of two themes. First, he let it be known he had the power to benefit the district, the schools and, especially, the board members through his position on the paper. He also had the power to harm them. Second, he had several prominent people endorse his position. One of the letters was from the lieutenant governor of the state. The letter was an obvious suggestion that the district could experience difficulty in getting the state funds it badly needed if the reporter's land was condemned.

The school board squirmed some, then knuckled under. It purchased another site that was far less suitable.

The reporter promptly doublecrossed the school board. He wrote only a few stories about the district after his victory. They were strongly—and unfairly—critical.

All of the pressure groups I have encountered have insisted that they were the people and that they made their demands in the name of the people and that they were interested only in benefiting the people and that their goal, whatever it happened to be, would, in fact, benefit the people. The first three claims never were true. The last was only rarely true.

Undeniably pressure groups do sometimes perform functions that are desirable for the community. I watched recently, for instance, a self-appointed, and quite vicious, watchdog over a city council make a demand for a contract change that saved the taxpayers of the city several thousand dollars. Another time a pressure group conducted a study on a location proposed by a school district engineer for a new school. The pressure group found another site that was better, cost less, and contained no homes that would have to be condemned and destroyed. Even the engineer involved finally admitted their site was

better and would save the taxpayers a neat piece of
money.

When I was in graduate school I made a study of
pressure groups. The research included interviewing people on both sides in five communities where
pressure groups were attempting or had attempted to
control either the city council or the school board. I
learned a lot. One of the more interesting things that
came to light was that while the members of the
pressure groups described themselves as unadul-
terated heroes fighting the forces of evil, the school
board and city council members did not entirely take
an opposite view. Often, they saw the pressure
groups as mixtures of good and evil. The elected officials in several cases pointed to specific programs of
the pressure groups that the elected officials felt had
resulted in benefits to the community. More generally, the elected officials unanimously believed that
the pressure groups' activities resulted in keeping the
elected officials "on their toes," an act which the officials saw as desirable from a community standpoint.

However, the elected officials also saw undesirable results of the pressure groups and most felt
that the undesirable results far outweighed the desirable ones.

In my observation the pressure groups cause the
officials to react to the groups' desires and needs
rather than to the general public's. The groups also,
almost always, perform with a viciousness that
deters many able people from serving in public office.
The people in official positions in the communities I
studied, for instance, found themselves being attacked in such a way that their standing in the community and sometimes their ability to earn a living
and even their health were affected.

Basically, the people who become part of pressure
groups can be divided into three types. First are the

crusaders, the people who see, sometimes quite accurately, a community need and seek the help of the legislative body involved.

Second are the profit seekers, the property owner who wants his street paved at the taxpayer's expense, for instance. Or the corporation that helps finance the congressman's election in hope of getting taxes shunted off to the working man. Or the lawyer who sees an opportunity to create a reputation and/or build a practice. Or a writer seeking a ready-made market. In short, anyone who sees a chance for profit.

Third is the pressure reliever. His goal is inside himself. He pretends to be working toward a community good of some sort, but his real motivation is a need to bring himself into the limelight, to build his ego, to project himself as a hero, or to harm people, most particularly, people in power. Often pressure relievers are simply bullies. They have found that they can, up to a point, slander and insult public officials with impunity. They can say things to a city council member, for example, that they can't say to anyone else without risk of being either struck or sued. The council member, because it is the tradition in this country, can only sit and listen while a citizen accuses him of any sort of crime or lack of integrity. A made-to-order situation for bullies.

Crusaders often conduct their campaigns alone or in small groups. When they have achieved their goal, or become convinced it cannot (or should not) be achieved, they disband and go away.

Profit seekers and pressure relievers often work together and enlist the aid of those crusaders they can convince that the goal would benefit the community. In order to persuade crusaders, profit seekers and pressure relievers conduct enormous and often effective propaganda campaigns. In the really

successful campaigns this has a snowballing effect.
Crusaders are persuaded by the propaganda to take
part in the campaign. They contribute money, time,
or ideas to the propaganda, thus helping enlist still
more crusaders, in addition to more profit seekers
and pressure relievers. That, in large measure, is
what has happened in the case of the major wilderness conservation groups.

There is a pattern, a series of stages, to the initi-
ation and growth of pressure groups. To some degree,
it is true of all of them, large or small. They follow
some variation of the pattern as they continue to
function and grow. When they do not run the full
course, it is because they stopped growing or ceased
to exist.

The pressure group begins with an individual or
small group, sometimes made up entirely of crusaders. In a situation where the community need is
obvious, urgent, and widespread, such as the need for
conservation of our land and resources, several
groups may spring up simultaneously. Eventually
they may merge, or at least work together.

As the pressure group becomes active it develops a
rude propaganda machine. That, if the goal has or
seems to have validity, attracts more members. Some
will be crusaders, others may be pressure relievers
who see the group as an opportunity to build their
egos, gain personal power, or vent their venom.
Others may be profit seekers who sense a potential
for acquisition.

Leadership develops in the group almost immediately. It is informal and so slight at first that it may
hardly be noticed. As the group grows, the leadership increases its strength and becomes more formal.

In the early stages the leadership consists probably
of one or more persons with strong personalities
making suggestions that are unthinkingly obeyed by

the others. With more than a handful of members, that no longer is sufficient. Leadership becomes more concrete, perhaps consisting of an individual who is consciously but informally acknowledged to be the leader. He may eventually delegate authority to subordinate leaders, then, as the group continues to grow, committees are appointed to divide the work load. Soon a formal constitution and bylaws are drawn up, the policy-making and administrative functions are shared by a president and a board of directors and there are elections.

Most groups never get beyond that stage. But some continue to grow until the volunteer leadership, no matter how tightly organized, no longer is sufficient. By this time dues and assessments have long been a part of the organization's discipline and there are funds available. A professional leader is hired.

At that moment the original purpose of the organization becomes secondary. The primary purpose from then on is to perpetuate the jobs of the professionals.

The people in power may maintain the appearance of a democratic framework by holding periodic elections, but by the time the professionals are in command, and usually long before, the establishment has control of the machinery of government and the finances. It uses those powers to build a strong internal propaganda machine. The leaders ask the members' opinion only in a contrived manner and in conjunction with a propaganda campaign designed to predetermine the outcome of any important plebiscite.

Discipline within the group grows apace with the size and formality of leadership. Light and informal at first, it becomes increasingly strict and formal with growth. Once the professionals take over, discipline is absolute.

The leaders are the disciplinarians. They deal quick punishment for even the slightest deviation from prescribed behavior. Punishment ranges from a slight frown to expulsion from the group. The severity depends on the standing of the miscreant, the importance of the infraction, and how threatening the infraction is to the people in power.

Regardless of appearances, the hierarchy keeps to itself all power. The power structure probably consists of the board of directors and officers and the professionals if there are any, the professionals dominating. Occasionally the board and officers are a false front and their apparent power actually lies in the hands of a behind-the-scenes individual or group. The professionals still dominate.

On rare occasions the members may revolt. Sometimes the revolution is successful and a new leadership takes over. Its members, however, will make only cosmetic changes. They will quickly replace the machine they overthrew with one of their own and, as far as the general membership is concerned, the dictatorship continues as before.

Such revolutions usually weaken and often destroy the parent organization. Usually that is well and good. The group has long since performed whatever benefit to society that it is going to and has become harmful to the community.

The wilderness conservation groups are among those that long since have performed the benefit to society they originally set out to perform. They have long since contributed to making the people and the government aware of the need for conservation of resources and the desirability of some land being set aside as declared wilderness. That awareness would have occurred anyway, but the pressure groups' propaganda certainly contributed to the process. The problem is that the country has become too aware, so aware that it tends to concentrate on those values to the exclusion of others just as important. Now that the hysterical period of the movement is subsiding, much of the nonwilderness parts of the movement are being re-examined and adjusted to conform to reality.

But perhaps because it is encased in law, administered by bureaucracy, and isolated from direct view by the public, the wilderness movement seems to have a momentum of its own, unaffected by the re-examination of related parts of the environmental movement. We still are overdoing the wilderness. We are setting aside so much land and so hugely over-protecting it that the program threatens to affect measurably the resources we have available. At the same time it is resulting in a danger that we will tremendously reduce citizens' opportunity to enjoy the natural surroundings of the forests and moun-tains on the public lands.

These overkills are in part caused by the fact that the wilderness conservation pressure groups cannot change their goals and tactics. They cannot change because they are largely controlled by profit seekers and pressure relievers whose interests are served by maintaining the program. To change would cause dissension in the ranks, reduction in membership and finances, organizational problems, loss of power and prestige. None of those results would be desirable from the point of view of the profit seekers and pres-sure relievers. So they use the group's internal propa-ganda apparatus to keep the membership whipped up and the goals unchanged, regardless of the needs of the community.

One of the results of the wilderness-conservation overkill is that the public is beginning to catch on. That could well result in a reaction that may destroy much of the good to which the wilderness conservation groups have contributed. It would be too bad, for instance, if the country reacted to too much land being locked up in wilderness by doing away with the wilderness program altogether.

CHAPTER THREE

Propaganda is an effort to sell an idea or doctrine. Despite its bad reputation, it is in a real sense a necessary part of democracy. Every political candidate engages in propaganda as he tries to sell himself and his platform. And every group that tries to spread its doctrine and principles does so through propaganda. In a way the advertising business uses propaganda to sell its merchandise. Ideas and goods would be difficult to move without propaganda. This book is propaganda aimed at slowing the headlong pace of wilderness declarations and so are the methods the publisher of the book uses to entice people to buy it.

There are tricks, of course, to propaganda (bias words, repetition, hiding the arguments against your doctrine, exaggeration, distortion, discrediting your opponents, and so forth). Some are unfair and unprincipled, but if both sides are fairly equal and have similar resources, they more or less balance each other out in bombast. The audience can sift through the counterarguments and come up with a reasonable facsimile of truth and on that truth base the right choice.

But the truth and right choice are dependent on both sides being reasonably able to present their rational arguments in balance, able to cancel out each other's bombast, bias words, distortions and un- truths.

It is when one side dominates that propaganda commits its crimes. Sometimes that occurs through force, as when a political dictator simply outlaws all doctrines but his own. It can also happen in a demo- cracy when a doctrine becomes so popular, so widely accepted that others are shut out. That happened with the environmental movement in the late 1960's and early 1970's. The environment message became gospel and its champions became saints. Neither was to be trifled with by prudent persons. By the mid- 1970's the pendulum had begun to swing the other way. The country was taking a second look at some of the more ridiculous (and more harmful) results of the earlier frenzy. But the wilderness movement, separated and isolated from direct contact with most Americans, was less affected by the reaction. Wil- derness environmentalists were as strong as ever.

Neither the wilderness pressure groups nor their tactics are unique. The groups follow a pattern of pressure groups everywhere in our society. An essen- tial part of that pattern is the attempt to obtain the power (pressure) to succeed in whatever their goal may be. Propaganda is a key tactic. The sophisti- cation of the propaganda varies with the sophisti- cation and resources of the pressure group. A hand- ful of traditionalists may try to force a school board

to throw out a textbook because it contains a word
they consider dirty. They probably will depend on a
few crude pamphlets plus the susceptibility of the
local media, and any editorial tricks they can dream
up, to get their name and their story out.

A large, well-heeled pressure group such as most
major conservation organizations probably will have
a much more sophisticated and versatile propaganda apparatus. (They tend, of course, to deny that they
are large, or powerful, or well heeled, or engage in
propaganda. But then, they also tend to deny they are
pressure groups.) Their propaganda begins with an
internal program designed to keep the members
interested, to maintain discipline, and to disseminate the party line. It keeps the members worked up
enough to take part in projects and submit dues and
donations. At the same time it is designed to prevent
the members from becoming so involved that they
question the leaders' goals, or methods.

The propagandists produce their printed internal
propaganda in newsletters, announcements, and so
forth. These messages go primarily to members but
also on occasion to nonmembers who are assumed to
be sympathetic to the cause.

One such was sent out in December 1974 to organize pressure on the U. S. Forest Service to establish
eleven more wilderness areas in the North Cascades
Mountains. Something like a million and a half acres
already were declared wilderness or National Park in
the North Cascades. Four more areas totaling 150,000
acres were formally designated to be studied for their
wilderness potential. The Forest Service a month
previously had held public meetings to make a preliminary report on a land-use study of the entire North
Cascades and to ask for public comment before
preparing a final draft. One alternative of the
preliminary plan set aside eleven more roadless areas

containing another 400,000 acres for possible future consideration as wilderness.

The preliminary plan actually included four alternatives. These could be combined to provide a reasonable, people-oriented plan providing for a continued supply of the raw material the forest furnishes, for recreation and even for more wilderness.

The wilderness conservation organizations would have none of it. Almost immediately after the Forest Service informational meeting six of the groups banded together to issue a four-page propaganda broadside.

The broadside was worded in the usual uncompromising, almost irrational style common to pressure groups' propaganda. The first sentence read: "Once again, the public must speak out for Washington wildlands, neglected by the Forest Service." The second paragraph told the faithful to "speak up for our shrinking wilderness."

The rest of the four pages were strongly worded support for the call-to-arms. The pamphlet completely ignored the compelling arguments against locking up more of the North Cascades. It did not allude to the loss of raw materials from forests and mines. It completely overlooked the fact that many of the things people like to do in the outdoors would be forbidden if the land were declared wilderness. Instead the prowilderness side was presented in emotional, contrived, and highly inflammatory language. All that was just window dressing, however. The faithful had long since been programmed to respond to the first two paragraphs, regardless of the contents of the rest of the pamphlet.

I attended one of the four public meetings. There were perhaps one hundred people there. Possibly ten of them were wilderness buffs. The others were horsemen, motorbikers, four-wheel drive enthusiasts, loggers, camping club members, hikers, hunters, fishermen, and so forth, all fearful that more of the public land would be declared wilderness and their activities restricted or prohibited.

The wilderness buffs were outnumbered ten to one in a meeting that was meant to produce ideas rather than a plebiscite. Despite that, the conservation groups banded together and published their pamphlet. The sole purpose of the pamphlet was to generate pressure that would force the Forest Service to accept their groups' dictates regardless of either reason or the majority will. They wanted the Forest Service to abandon its program of putting the land to its best uses, to best serve the most people. Instead, they wanted the land devoted exclusively to their own interests. That, in itself, is probably not a great social ill. Democracy can handle blind selfishness. The problem is that these groups are so well organized and so wealthy and powerful they may well be able to push their program through, despite reason or the will of the majority.

The North Cascade pamphlet was a single-purpose, one-time publication. Conservation groups also distribute regular, periodic publications for in-house consumption. (I don't mean to imply that all conservation publications are of the same ilk. Indeed, some of them are intellectually edited and make an honest attempt to present the issues in proper perspective and with all sides honestly put forth.) An example of the extremes to which such publications can go is *Not Man Apart* which bears on its cover the declaration "Published for Friends of the Earth, League of Conservation Voters, Friends of the Earth Foundation." Inside, it lists David Brower as president of Friends of the Earth, president of Friends of the Earth Foundation, and member of League of Conservation Voters.

The publication is typical of the standard, raw-propaganda methods that have existed at least since the invention of the movable-type printing press. The issue of December 1974 is typical.[1] This twenty-page publication is printed on newsprint in tabloid format. It comes in the mail folded in half. On the front cover is a photograph of four 1920-era bathing beauties on a motorboat with the United States flag flying full-spread behind the foremost bathing beauty. On the back cover is a note signed by David Brower saying that "the cost of saving the earth has gone up," and announcing that the organization is raising its dues. Cost of basic membership is going from $15 to $20.

Below the note are two coupons for persons wishing to renew their membership or give a gift membership. They list seven categories of membership ranging from student member at $7.50 a year to patron, $5,000 or more.

Inside the tabloid are photographs, drawings, articles, letters to the editor, reviews, poems, and so forth. There are only two themes. The first extols Friends of the Earth, its designs, and people who boost them. The second satirizes, insults, and vilifies those who disagree.

The publication describes enemies and unacceptable ideas with sarcasm and ill humor. Those pages describing good guys and their actions are much sweeter but far fewer. Friends of the Earth appears to have more hates than loves.

There are pieces maligning lumber companies, the oil industry, tourists, Expo 74 World Fair,[2] nuclear energy, dams, log trucks, television programs about the outdoors, and so forth. Other pieces praise Friends of the Earth, *Not Man Apart*, a television spot produced by FOE Foundation and featuring singer Janis Ian, and two books, one by Kenneth

Brower who is identified, in the last paragraph, as a son of David Brower.

Intellectually it is all very crude, of course. But it is highly effective as a tool for keeping the troops fired up and ready to respond thoughtlessly and uncritically to whatever commands the hierarchy issues.

As a matter of fact one column titled *Friends of the Earth Workshop* urges readers to write to congressmen to let them know in advance that they will hear from readers and FOE's Washington staff (i.e. lobby) whenever bills that concern conservation are to be considered by Congress.

One of the programs the congressmen will have thus forcefully brought to their attention, the column intimates, is an opportunity to create almost 100 million acres of wilderness, parks, and wildlife refuges within the following two years.

The message of the publication is quite clear. All earth will cease to exist unless humanity immediately and unquestioningly adopts the economic and political institutions advocated by Friends of the Earth. But if humanity obeys, peace and serenity will reign. Just who is going to run this worldwide Utopia isn't spelled out, but it isn't too difficult to guess.

Conservation groups don't rely entirely on publications to keep the faithful fired up. Not the least of their tools are the meetings of chapters, organizations, and groups. Such meetings provide an opportunity for the leadership to exhort the faithful on a face-to-face basis. The printed material, of course, reaches a larger audience, but the face-to-face meetings give a personal touch that make them by far the more persuasive.

Nearly all kinds of pressure groups, conservationists included, hold membership meetings. The big show, however, is the convention in which members of the various groups come together for a mammoth, international, granddaddy of meetings.

The *Herald* sent me to a conservation convention a few years ago in Seattle. It was billed as the Tenth Biennial Northwest Wilderness Conference. I've been to some conferences but this one was an experience, a lesson in folk manipulation that should be witnessed by every American.

The three-day affair was staged in a large hall at the Seattle Center. About eight hundred people showed up. Most of them could be sharply divided into the customary two distinct types. The largest group was the well-to-do elite, the people, mostly middle-aged, who wore casual but expensive clothes, used rough language in a refined way, and were ostentatiously accustomed to moderate affluence and comfort. The other group were young, long-haired, and dressed in cheap and ragged clothing. They, too, used rough language, but they were more inclined to use it in a rough manner. Their ostentation was a disdain for affluence and comfort.

Superficially, the two types are completely dissimilar as far as wealth is concerned, but they have one strong bond. Both have reached or are assured they will reach the level of affluence they want. If they have ever had to struggle to accumulate worldly goods, they are through with that struggle now. Now they are interested in places to play.

But that was only part of the reason they were there. The advance literature for the meeting had made a strong point of listing the names of more than two dozen wilderness-conservation celebrities who would attend. The list was headed by Nathaniel Reed, Assistant Secretary of Interior for Parks and Wildlife and Floyd K. Haskell, U. S. senator from Colorado, chairman, Subcommittee on Public Lands.

The rest of the list read like a Who's Who of the conservation hierarchy. There were presidents, executive directors, coordinators, representatives, trustees, pioneers and past presidents of about every wilderness conservation group I had ever heard of and several that I hadn't.

As the meeting progressed it was interesting to watch how the common members flocked deferentially around the leaders. It was easy to see that these celebrities were the cocks of the wilderness conservation roost. They had come to instill new fervor and vigor in the followers and to be admired.

And plainly their audience had come to be in the presence of these idols, to breathe the same air, to hear, to be inspired, and to worship. Obviously many of those who crowded around the golden ones were hoping some of the glory would rub off. The golden ones, of course, were humble, speaking and smiling benignly, shaking hands, allowing their radiance to shine on all who approached.

Of course, many of those in attendance were not profit seekers or pressure relievers. Many, I believe, were crusaders, filled with zeal to save the world from evil forces. They had accepted the propaganda line and were at least temporarily beyond the point of questioning the leaders, their goals, or their motives. They were there only to hear the great ones utter truth and to learn how the world must be saved.

Another type was present. A comparatively small group whom I felt the more sorry about because some of them are friends of mine. They were the people from the National Park Service and the Forest Service. There must have been twenty of them, ranging from middle management level to pretty high. They had been summoned and, even though I happen to know at least some of them are aware of the excesses

involved in the wilderness conservation crusade,
they came. They came because few people in government service have the courage to stand up to the
awesome power of the wealth, lobbies, and propaganda represented at that convention.

The convention organizers had summoned the
government officials to prove they had the power to
do so. How better to impress the members? The
presence of the officials demonstrated that the organizers could command people who administer the
public land. That, by implication, meant they had the
power to command those administrators' decisions.
How better to demonstrate that the pressure groups
were well led and effective? How better to keep
interested and loyal the pressure relievers at the
convention? How better to demonstrate the success
and the power of the wilderness group, impress members and awe opponents?

The convention leaders made the most of it. The
master of ceremonies called in a dull, disinterested
voice on the park and forest people during the intro-
duction ceremonies. He called them one by one to
stand and be recognized. It was much like the ancient
kings parading their captives before the mobs after a
battle to demonstrate the power and prowess of the
rulers. And, like the rejoicing mobs of the ancient city
states, the audience in Seattle cheered—lightly—as
each man, in his turn, was displayed.

And that, really, was one of the high points of the
conference. The celebrities gave speeches with high-
sounding titles, or took part in panels. There was a
round table titled *Getting Through the Political
Thicket—What Works and What Doesn't*. It was designed to teach conferees how to bring pressure on
government agencies. There was a film festival of
party-line flavor and an exhibit of displays. During

the social intermissions the faithful clustered around whatever celebrities happened to be available. I listened. The conversations often centered on the conferees' admiration for each other and hate for the "corporate minds," an appellation that covers all non-believers. There was also an abundance of pamphlets produced by the conservation groups represented. They passed them out with great zeal but I noticed that several of the litter cans conspicuously placed around the conference room were nearly full of them long before the conference ended.

But despite the long agenda and the long sessions, the basic reason for the conference was to allow the conferees to see and speak, to be seen and be heard by each other. And thereby to be filled with zeal to go out and save the world. And to be reassured by each other that theirs was the only road to salvation.

The conference was well planned and well executed. No doubt, almost everyone left fully inspired to fearlessly do whatever the leadership might see fit to command. Unquestioningly, of course.

A key to all propaganda, including the internal propaganda of wilderness conservation pressure groups, is the use of biased language. Even the crudest propagandist soon learns that he can sway people by using pleasant words to support his arguments and ugly words to describe the other side. That is natural and normal and not even necessarily undesirable as long as the propaganda on both sides is close enough to being equal so they cancel each other out. If each side calls the other names, the onlooker is constrained to make his decisions on the strength of their arguments rather than the strength of their epithets. All the pressure groups I have encountered have used bias words as part of their propaganda technique, none more cleverly or less fairly than the wilderness conservationists. Even a partial lexicon of the bias words they use most frequently should give an idea of how they work the system:

Unique—Anything wilderness conservationists want declared wilderness.
   It is the last (only) one on earth,
   they say, and once it is gone,
   it will be gone forever. (They are
   quite right, of course. Nature
   never duplicates itself
   exactly, so everything
   is unique.)
Uncomparable—Same as unique.
Incomparable—Same as uncomparable.
Environment—What they are for and everyone
   else is against.
Ecology—Same as environment.
Lush—What all wildlife and vegetation are.
The People—Conservation groups and their
   supporters. Good guys. Often stated as
   "Us."
Citizens—Same as The People.
Corporations—Everyone else. Bad guys.
   Often stated as "They."
Special Interests—Same as corporations.
Wildlife—What will be destroyed if conser-
   vation groups are not given everything
   they want.
Bureaucracy—Government agents who
   don't obey wilderness conservation
   groups' commands. Or,
   are slow to.

Friends—Government agents who obey
conservation groups' commands.
Quickly.

De Facto Wilderness—Land they want
declared wilderness they describe
as being wilderness de facto (in fact)
but not yet officially declared so by
law. This would apply to Times
Square on Manhattan Island if they
wanted it. And, indeed,
they may.

Oblivion—The opposite of wilderness.

Litter—What people do when they
are allowed to visit someplace.
(Except wilderness conservationists,
of course. Conservationists don't
litter.)

Pristine—What something will remain if it
is given to the conservationists. The
term can apply to annual plants a few
months old or a rock billions of years
old.

Primordial—*Same as* pristine.

Primitive—*Same as* primordial.

Uncorrupted—*Same as* primitive.

Esthetic Value—What conservationists
appreciate and everyone else does not.

Roadless—What land they want is or should
be.

Virgin—A reason land they want should be
made wilderness—to protect its virginity.

Untouched—*Same as* virgin.

Beautiful—*Same as* untouched.

Majestic—*Same as* beautiful.

Barren—What land they want will become if
they don't get it. What land they don't

have has become because they didn't get
it.

Delicate—Any land they want may be described as delicate. And, of course, it
must be given to them so they can protect
it.

Natural—A value they approve of.

Spiritual—*Same as* natural.

Scars—Anything man has done is a scar. A
road is a scar, a trail is a scar, a
building is a scar, a trail sign is a
scar.

Varied—The reasons for their campaigns.

Singleminded—The reasons for everyone
else's campaigns.

Selfless—Their motives.

Selfish—Everyone else's motives.

Save—What they do to land.

Protect—*Same as* save.

Preserve—*Same as* protect.

Destroy—What everyone else does to land.

Rape—*Same as* destroy.

Vandalize—*Same as* rape.

Threaten—*Same as* vandalize.

Love—What they feel for land and nature.

Careless—What everyone else feels for
land and nature.

Anger (Righteous)—What they feel toward
corporations.

Weak, Poor—Themselves.

Powerful, Rich—Everyone else.

Sadness—What wilderness conservationists
feel for civilization if they don't get
their way.

Hope—What wilderness conservationists
feel for civilization if they do get
their way.

Enlightened—Themselves.

Ignorant—Everyone else.

Intrude—What people do on land wilderness
conservationists want set aside for
themselves. (Except conservationists,
of course. Conservationists
don't intrude.)

Stewardship—What they feel toward land,
wildlife, vegetation, and humanity.

Indifference—What everyone else feels
toward land, wildlife, vegetation, and
humanity.

Incredible (Incredibly)—Adjective (adverb)
used to emphasize any of above.

In addition to a lexicon of bias words, the wilderness-conservation propagandists have formulas they follow for describing things. For instance, when they describe a place they want assigned to themselves, they begin by naming it, then apply some positive bias words, then list it real or imagined attributes, then imply that those attributes are threatened by something, and apply negative bias words to the threat. Thus, they might say something like:

Boulder Mountain, that unique, majestic, virgin mountain stands beautiful, with its incredibly thick forest of Douglas fir, western red cedar, hemlock, and silver fir towering over lush meadows of blue lupine, ruby Indian paint brush, red huckleberry, white Indian pipe, purple fireweed, yellow tiger lily, and pale beargrass. But, below, at the end of delicate valleys that radiate from this untouched giant of primordial beauty, barren black ribbons of asphalt scar the landscape where Highway 250731 carries its ugly,

gas-guzzling, smoke-belching cars full of gawk-
ing tourists who indifferently toss their litter to
the roadside threatening the majesty of the
mountain with rape and destruction. And within
the protective forest, screened from the destructive highway, live the wildlife, the deer, the
antelope, the cuddly black bear, the grey wolf,
the furry beaver and the aloof rattlesnake, little
knowing the threat of destruction that lies at the
end of the forest they have known since time
began.

The implication is clear. All those good things will
disappear and all those bad things will spread unless
The People act quickly.

An extremely effective propaganda technique, wilderness conservationists use it over and over again.
It is especially valuable to them because its effect is
by implication and they can't be maneuvered into
defending it. If someone questions them on the facts,
they can simply shrug and say that isn't what they
meant.

The conservation groups' internal propaganda has
been highly successful. It has kept the troops fired up
and uncritical of the leadership. That in turn gives
the leaders a cadre of people who, while they are only
a tiny fraction of the population, speak with one
voice. That voice sounds as if the vast majority of
Americans were speaking.

The existence of the cadre provides the leaders
with a number of people who will write letters, sign
petitions, and make statements simply because the
leaders tell them to. Thus, the pressure groups can
within a short period have a congressman or
administrator deluged with letters and personal con-
tacts and phone calls that will convince him he is
hearing the voice of the public.

Since the people with views different from the conservation leaders are unorganized, they find it difficult to make their voice heard, no matter how they try. If they do begin to be heard, they find themselves becoming a target of the insults and verbal offenses of the pressure group leaders and their automatons.

CHAPTER FOUR

The pressure group propagandist has a relatively easy task in producing internal propaganda. He knows who his audience is and how to reach it. He can depend on his audience to accept uncritically and unquestioningly almost anything he says.

External propaganda is a somewhat more difficult task. There, the assignment is not just to keep fires burning in the breasts of people who already are faithful believers. Instead, the propagandist faces a whole new audience, unsold and perhaps even skeptical of the pressure group's easy solutions.

The propagandist has two goals in his external production. First, he wants to recruit new members. Second, he wants to confuse the issues with the non-members so, if they are not with him, at least they won't oppose him.

Specifically, for the wilderness conservation group

propagandists, the object is to make their party line
and projects the "in" things. If the propagandists
make it seem that theirs is the sole solution and the
only enlightened approach to problems, they have
gained immense momentum. Then they are likely to
have their programs touted unthinkingly at cocktail
parties and family picnics by people who know
nothing about the subject but simply need something to talk about to keep up their end of the conversation. Such people can assume that their conversation partners know no more than they do, so they
repeat the propaganda they have heard, secure in the
knowledge that no one will refute them. Thus the
pressure groups' wilderness propaganda is spread
through places like Queens, New York, and Chicago
by people who know nothing about wilderness.
Knowing discussions about mountains and forests
are initiated by people who have never visited mountains and forests, never will visit them and if they
did, wouldn't have the background to understand
what they saw. They parrot the pressure groups'
propaganda, believing that because they have read it
so often, it must be true. And thus they unwittingly
become a part of that propaganda.

A society develops from time to time unquestionable concepts, ideas that are accepted generally
because they are generally accepted. They become so
much a part of the society's collective thinking that
they cannot be questioned. A study a few years ago
indicated that the Japanese attack on Pearl Harbor
was successful because the society of military people
in Hawaii believed it couldn't happen. Some individuals understood that it could, that, indeed, the
island was quite vulnerable to attack. But they
remained silent because the unspoken dictum of that
society at that time was that a successful attack on
Pearl Harbor could not even be considered possible

by intelligent people. Anyone who broke that unspoken rule would be silenced by laughter, ridicule, or other social retribution. So no one spoke out. And, of course, the impossible happened.

That sort of unspoken dictum is what the wilderness pressure groups have brought about through their propaganda machines. They have achieved a situation in which anyone who speaks at all about wilderness must parrot the pressure groups' concepts and programs. Anyone who disagrees, or even questions, is put down as a mercenary representative of commercial interests, one who speaks for industry, and everyone knows that industry is intent only on destroying the wilderness for greedy profits. People who disagree aloud find themselves ridiculed and insulted. Most unbelievers simply keep silent. And the pressure groups' propaganda rolls on uninhibited.

The overwhelming power of the wilderness-conservation groups is not due solely to their propaganda. A variety of social and economic trends focus the nation's attention on them. Among the trends are the rise in power of the military-industrial complex. President Eisenhower publicly warned the nation to be wary of it in the early 1960s, about the time the wilderness-conservation groups were building their power base. That gave enormous impetus to their anti-industrial doctrines.

The end of America's free-land era also provided a weapon in the conservationists' arsenal. The era really had ended long ago but the nation's habits and attitudes still were based on a belief that problems could be solved by moving west. We had run out of west and the people were just beginning to feel the effects. That gave the wilderness-conservationists the opportunity to suggest that their plan somehow would preserve some of the dead past.

Then, too, the wilderness conservation movement received impetus from the fact that technology had grown so fast and so large that it threatened to overwhelm society. The advent of instant information, worldwide communication, the addition of thinking machines to the hoard of working machines we hadn't fully assimilated, longer life spans, the disintegration of institutions that began before history— all these forces and many more made the social scene ripe for anything that promised relief.

Declaring segments of land to be wilderness could not really provide that relief but with adroit propaganda it could be made to seem to, and the pressure groups took advantage of that.

Concern over the growth of technology and loss of the free-land frontier were not new to the mid-twentieth century. Ben Franklin and Thomas Jefferson both foresaw problems. In the 1880s Frederick Jackson Turner built a career as the nation's leading historian almost entirely on his recognizing that the frontier was being used up and on describing the effect that would have on American society.

Nor was the battle over wilderness new in the 1970's. More than a half century earlier John Muir and Gifford Pinchot were clawing at each other's throats over how much of the public lands should be locked up.[1]

But if none of the forces that created the wilderness-conservation groups were new, they all were growing and in mid-twentieth century they coalesced to become overwhelmingly dominant.

The catalyst of that coalition was the wilderness-conservation groups' external propaganda. The propagandists developed two major tools to disseminate their program—books and the news media. They use both with exquisite skill.

For instance: Not long ago I interviewed two young men who were traveling around the world by foot, paddle, and sail. They meant, they said, to use no mechanical means of transportation at all. That seemed pretty ambitious but they already had walked 2,900 miles from Alaska to Everett in six months and they said they expected to devote ten years to the trip. They looked pretty tough; I guess if Marco Polo could survive his trip, they might make theirs.

During the interview I asked them what the purpose of their trip was. They were, they said, environmentalists and they were using the trip as a means for publicizing the need for environmental awareness. One method was to drop in at newspapers along the way and tell of environmental problems in the neighborhood. As an example, they said, when they were approaching Everett in a canoe that morning they had detected the smell of the paper mills in Everett's industrial area. That smell, they said, meant the air was being poisoned and they asked the conservation groups' stock question, "What right does industry have to poison the air we breathe?"

"How do you know it is poison?" I asked.

They seemed startled. "We smelled it."

"How do you know what you smelled is poison?"

"Of course it is poison."

I told them Everett's air was monitored by the Environmental Protection Agency but they rejected the statement simply by shaking their heads.

"That's the trouble with industry," one of the young men said. "It doesn't care."

That Everett's paper mills were in the process of spending tens of millions of dollars to eliminate the smell they objected to was a fact they rejected, too.

The young men went on to tell of other environ-

mental impacts they had seen on their hike and
repeated the conservationists' stock scare phrases
about destruction of the environment and extinction
of the human race unless we control our interference
with nature.

I asked if the laws that require environmental
impact statements didn't control our interference
with nature. It turned out they had never heard of
environmental impact statements and didn't know
what they were. Neither were they aware of the work
of the federal Environmental Protection Agency or of
similar units on the state level. They seemed not to
know about the laws that prohibit industrial pollution and require earlier pollution to be cleaned up. I
mentioned those facts but the young men were not
impressed. They still insisted that society was heed-
less of the environment. They criticized all the things
conservation groups are critical of, mining, logging—
especially clearcut logging—industry, petroleum, the
automobile. My questions frustrated and finally
angered them. One told me I was just too backward
to understand their message and they were wasting
their time. He threatened to leave.

I liked them and they had a good story so I backed
off and finished the interview with less difficult
questions. The story ran on top of page one. However, Supreme Court Justice Douglas, who a few
years earlier had made the same kind of statements
about mining and logging only a few miles from
Everett, had a stroke that day. The Douglas story
came through at the last minute and the desk cut out
a third of the story about the young men to make
room for the Justice.

The basic truths of the young men's observations
are undeniable, of course. Technology has obviously
given man the tools to destroy himself in many ways.
But they had only the vaguest notions of the dangers

and they were completely naive about society's response to the dangers. Lacking knowledge, they relied on the pat solutions of the wilderness conservation pressure groups.

They smelled something from Everett's pulp mills and automatically decided it was poison. Their response would be to shut down Everett's paper mills and, by inference, all paper mills everywhere. A paperless society would cease to function, but if they had faced that fact, they didn't mention it.

When they left Everett, the two young men were headed south, toward Mexico, where they were to write a book to finance the rest of their adventure. They said Friends of the Earth was one of their sponsors and they hoped that organization would publish their book.

I have spent a good part of my life in the back country, but frankly, even the part of the trip before they cross the ocean (in a canoe or sailboat from South America to Africa) sounds more than a little scary. Even so, the two are young and tough, adaptable and determined. If anyone can make it, they can. I hope they do.

One problem is that they both seemed intelligent and by the time they reach Mexico they may have begun to see through the simplistic arguments of the wilderness conservation groups they worship. That would be a shame. Once they lose their youthful naiveté, once they begin to question, they will be of no value to wilderness-conservationists. It will, I'm afraid, become more difficult for them to find a publisher for their book.

If they do write the book for Friends of the Earth, I think I know what it will be like. Except for style and anecdotes, it will be pretty much a duplicate of a recent book by Michael Frome.[2] A typical environmental writer, Frome has memorized the policies, programs, and dictates of the wilderness-conser-vation establishment and he has learned a seemingly infinite number of ways to express them. In his acknowledgments, Frome tells us the idea for the book was broached to him by the Wilderness Society but, he says, the society bosses did not interfere while he was writing it. Of course not. The Wilder-ness Society knew exactly what he would write.

I began to wonder in the early part of the book when Frome seems to say that he learned about nature by looking at the stars while navigating an airplane during World War II. I was a private in a Marine Corps artillery outfit during that war so it probably is natural that I would be suspicious of anything that flew. But disregarding my natural prejudices, I can't see how riding on soft cushions in an aluminum bird thousands of feet in the air at hun-dreds of miles an hour pushed by hundreds of horse-power could give someone an insight into nature or wilderness.

Not that I disagree with everything Frome says in his book. For instance, he says the country should view its land as a total system rather than on a piece-by-piece basis.[3] I'm not sure he realized that implies dividing the public lands among all the people rather than giving it exclusively to his powerful sponsors. Whatever he meant, I couldn't agree more with his words.

But if there were a few places in the book where I smiled, there were many more where I couldn't help frowning. One part of the book that is especially distasteful is his criticism of the National Park Ser-vice for proposing tramways in the North Cascades National Park[4] where I spend much of my time both working and playing.

After Congress created the park in 1968, the Park Service devised a plan for developing it. The plan actually mentioned three tramways but only the one on Ruby Peak ever really was given serious consideration.

Frome faults the tramway on the grounds that it would lead to commercial development at the base and that park visitors from the lowlands would ride it in light clothing and thin shoes, risking the possibility of being trapped in a sudden blizzard.

Nothing in his book indicates Frome has ever seen Ruby Peak. That, I suppose, gives me an advantage. I have not only climbed it but walked its trails—all of them, I think—camped on its benches and shoulders and in the valleys beside it. I've boated on Ross Lake at its foot. I've seen it from the top and the sides and below and from the peaks of half a dozen neighboring mountains. It seems to me a perfect place for a tramway.

To begin with, what Frome doesn't say is that Ruby Peak is not in the National Park proper but in the Ross Lake Recreation Area which is adjacent to the park and managed by the park but not as a wilderness. One reason Ruby Peak is part of a recreation area instead of part of the park is that the North Cascades Highway—one of the state's major east-west roads—borders two sides of its base.

Actually the proposed location of the tramway is on a shoulder of the mountain between the highway and Ross Lake. There is barely room for the tramway base let alone the concession, snack bar, restaurant, lodge, cocktail lounge, souvenir shop, electric power, water lines, sewage disposal, employees' quarters, and bulldozers that Frome says probably would follow development of a tramway. There will be little enough room for the tram and its parking lot. It seems unlikely any of the other amenities will be located there. More's the pity. The base of Ruby Peak seems a highly suitable place for all of them—assuming, of course, that the bulldozers go away when their job is done.

And why not? The plan is to have the tram go up the mountainside in two stages with an interpretive center and nature trails at both terminals. Visitors then can see and have explained the mountain's natural wonders and how they change with elevation.

The tramway would provide an educational opportunity equal to many hours of study in the dry atmosphere of a college lecture hall, an educational opportunity that should be available to every American. And since there is no such tramway anywhere in Washington State's portion of the Cascade Range and since Ruby Peak seems like a perfect place, why not?

Frome's warning about people being caught in a blizzard is preposterous. If a sudden blizzard came up—not all that likely, really—the people would simply leave the interpretative centers and nature trails, get back on the tramway and ride down the mountain.

Weak points abound in the book. Frome suggests, for instance, that clearcut logging and road building make places useless for recreation, that even archeological sites should be sacrificed to wilderness, that the "principal alternative" to wilderness is crowds, noise, and mechanical contrivances, that only commercial interests are opposed to the wilderness groups, that the U. S. Park Service is wrong when it argues that its "parks are for people," and so on. He even suggests that the grizzly bear originally was not hostile but that it changed from being a docile animal to its present ferocious nature, apparently, only because civilization appeared on the scene.[5] (If so, it happened with amazing suddenness since Lewis and Clark ran into some specimens that impressed even their adventurous souls.)

Frome's book is only one among the many

wilderness conservation books. They are written in different styles and from different approaches, of course, but they have the same purpose: to sell a one-sided version of the wilderness program. They vary from plain prose like Frome's to poetry and to photos-and-captions, but their purpose is always the same, to repeat the well-rehearsed party line, to gain recruits for the wilderness groups, and to cause enough doubt in the minds of nonbelievers so they will not interfere with the wilderness groups' pressure on the governmental agencies involved. They have had, unfortunately, far more success than is good for society as a whole.

Books are an important part of the wilderness-conservation groups' external propaganda. An equally important role has been played by news-papers and radio-TV stations that have—knowingly or not—allowed themselves to be manipulated by the wilderness conservationists.

Manipulation of the media is not new, of course. It began almost simultaneously with the invention of movable type when European kings required printers to print only approved information.

That crude form of censorship is still exercised by governments in many parts of the world. But the system has grown and become more sophisticated with time. Now the pressures on newsmen are myriad and often extremely subtle.

There are many kinds of newsmen. None, I suppose, is typical, but there are some things that most of us have in common. We are, for instance, nearly all college graduates. Many of us went to jour-nalism school which, we are convinced, gives the best training to reporters. Others majored in some-thing else and are convinced that is the best training. We nearly all finished a four-year course. Some took two-year courses. There are still a few reporters with no college at all. They sometimes become good but they are, I suspect, an endangered species.

We once were nearly all middle-class, white Americans, but that is changing. When I started in the business, the typical reporter was supposed to be hard-drinking, cynical, and somewhat unstable. That was never completely true. It is even less so now, but some do fit that stereotype. And many people continue to hold that image of us.

We have the same thought patterns and mental characteristics as the rest of humanity. We have paranoia, suspicion, trust, greed, charity, intelligence, ability, talent, and stupidity on the same scale as do people of other callings. We share the same prejudices as many other people and on the full scale. I, for instance, believe that most public officials are capable and honest. On the other hand, I once knew a reporter who believed all people in government are both incompetent and dishonest. Once she told me she considered herself a failure because she had been covering a city hall for two years and had not been able to uncover any skulduggery. It was government and she was sure the people involved belonged in jail. She felt inadequate because she had not been able to prove anything despite two years of trying.

She still hasn't uncovered anything, but she's still trying.

As they do with other people, our prejudices come from many sources. Some we inherit. Others come from our environment. Some we carry all our lives. Others come and go. All of us are subject to the prejudices of our times. If, because of social and propaganda pressures, much of our society is convinced of the truth or untruth of a concept, we will share that conviction on about the same scale as the rest of the population.

That is what has happened in the case of the wilderness-conservation movement. A part of the population as a whole and journalism in particular have been persuaded by the ubiquitous propaganda that the movement is against all the things that are bad for society and for all the things that are good for society. They are likely to believe, also, that only greedy evildoers would oppose the movement. Like some of the general public, some reporters assume truth on the part of the movement and untruth on the part of all others in the same way that they assume tomorrow's sun will rise in the east.

The people who hold such prejudices tend to be interested in the topics involved. Since editors tend to assign reporters to beats and stories in which they are interested, it is likely that a writer assigned to a highly volatile subject will be prejudiced about it. Not all reporters who cover the wilderness conservation movement are prejudiced, but some are.

Long ago, when I was a journalism undergraduate, young reporters were taught to recognize and compensate for their prejudices, to give both sides in a news story that is not labeled as opinion. In some quarters, at least, that practice seems to have become old hat. Many young journalists are coming into the business obsessed with the idea that they know what is good and right. Their responsibility, they believe, is to persuade, not just to inform.

Some journalism professors now teach what is called "new journalism." To some, that means writing outside of the traditional journalistic forms such as the inverted pyramid and 5-Ws formulas, to let the story determine the form rather than to stick to rigid convention. To others, new journalism means telling only those parts of the story that conform to the writer's prejudice. Sometimes that process is called "advocacy journalism." If it is not labeled as such, it is not honest, and I fear that label is lacking more now than it once was.

Some reporters from all the various media are apt to slant their stories, but radio and television reporters are more susceptible because of their time limitations. Their advantage is that they can get information to the consumer before we newspaper people even get back to our desks to write the story. Their disadvantage is that their whole news broadcast contains fewer words than our front page. They have to ignore most of the stories we run routinely. The stories they do run are boiled down to just a few sentences. That is barely enough for the highlights and the temptation to choose the highlights that conform to their prejudices is too strong to be denied by some.

In addition to those who are unable or unwillling to subjugate their prejudices, some reporters are simply incompetent. The result is that in some cases the reader cannot trust what he reads in the news columns of his paper or hears on the news broadcasts. That is not really frequent on a relative basis, but, still it happens more than it should.

All reporters, of course, make mistakes. And all media occasionally inadvertently allow those mistakes to get into the news reports. But the prejudiced and incompetent reporters produce misinformation or distorted information far more regularly than normal. And some newspapers and broadcast stations are more likely than others to harbor such reporters. For instance, the Associated Press obtains most of its news from reporters on its customer or member papers and stations. I have it on good authority that at least one AP bureau maintains a list of newsrooms and individual reporters whose stories it won't use until they have been thoroughly verified. "Once we've been burned a few times," my source said, "we make it a point to check very thoroughly on stories from certain sources."

As a reporter who is proud of his craft, I am not happy to acknowledge that there are prejudiced and incompetent journalists. Not many, but more than is good for either journalism or society.

Reporters have other characteristics. All, or nearly all, reporters are storytellers, entertainers. It does no good to publish information unless it is read. So we try to make it as interesting as possible. Occasionally that means twisting something a little. Some reporters do that routinely. And I suspect we all let it happen once in a while.

That leads us into the "good story" syndrome. In some newsrooms the term "good story" has become passé. Still, all reporters are continually on the hunt for the kind of story that will be widely read, the kind that editors will put on page one with a big headline, the kind that other media may copy. Reporters compete both with reporters on opposition media and with reporters who work in the same newsroom. It is a score, a mark of success, to have your story played better than others. Sometimes we are tempted to overemphasize or eliminate a fact to improve a story.

Our hunt for a "good story" causes both reporters and editors to tend to fall into patterns on the subjects we publish. We love contention and struggle. A legislative meeting in which there is controversy and namecalling will often receive more attention than one in which important decisions are made. We like any kind of violence and bloodshed. Some papers devote large proportions of their reporting energy to covering fires, shootings, crime, accidents, or the like. There even are loose formulas for equating the amount of violence with the amount of reporters' energy devoted to it. An automobile accident with only a minor injury, for instance, may be overlooked entirely. A passenger plane accident with hundreds of fatalities may be assigned to nearly all the available reporters and occupy several prominent pages.

Especially if it happens nearby. A single fatality in
the home town is more important than a double fatality in the next town.

We also like natural calamities such as storms,
earthquakes, tornadoes, and blizzards, which we
usually describe as "paralyzing." Often we run pictures and descriptions of the worst segment of such
calamities and let the reader suppose that represents
the entire scene. We have been doing that so long that
most readers are aware of it. Some disbelieve our
disasters even when they are real.

Some of our pattern stories repeat themselves.
Reporters are always on the lookout for stories about
the end of the world and of the human race. Sometimes the catastrophe is predicted by a religious
fanatic. He finds in the Bible that doom is imminent.
He gets a story in the paper. Then, as a follow story,
he finds that he can give an exact date. The date
arrives and doom fails. So he discovers he made a
miscalculation. He provides another date. Another
story. Again the date arrives but the end of the world
does not. Everyone loses interest. Until the next pro-
phet arrives.

At other times the doom is predicted by scientists.
Sometimes humanity is threatened with extinction
because the climate is becoming warmer. Sometimes
because it is becoming cooler. Sometimes wetter and
sometimes drier. Many papers have carried all these
predictions down the years and many times over.

We also repeat endlessly such "good stories" as the
"polar bear clubs" which allow us to take pictures of
their members diving into a local body of water at
midwinter. And there is the "long hiker" who has
walked, or is going to walk a long distance, or as a
variation, rides a bike or horse or pushes a
wheelbarrow.

We love epidemics almost as much as bloodshed,

and we usually will run stories when they are predicted, when they arrive, and when they end. The play they get depends on how many people will die, are dying, and did die and how close to home they will be, are and were.

We also love records and championships of almost any kind. Sportswriters, especially, are always inventing phony records that sound something like "the most two-base hits by a left-handed batter more than twenty-six years old who was an Eagle Scout and keeps pythons in the bathroom since 1947." I actually have seen stories about champion eaters of clams, pies, corn on the cob, and live goldfish. And we have had record numbers of people crowded into Volkswagens and phone booths. Once I saw on television a picture of the record number of people who held each others' hands while doing a midair forward somersault on skis. And once I saw a story about the record number of people who held hands in a ring after they jumped out of airplanes but before they opened their parachutes.

Then, too, we like the unusual and unexpected. "It is not news when a dog bites a man. It is news when a man bites a dog," an editor once said and reporters have been looking for a man with his teeth in a dog's rump ever since. Or, as a variation, someone with a mouthful of lion or skunk.

Once one reporter has "scored" with a "good story," it is likely to be repeated over and over. The first story in the 1930s about a college kid eating a live goldfish was followed by stories from campuses all over the country. Each story contained a "record" of more goldfish eaten than on the last campus. Then as goldfish became old hat (or scarce) the stories covered other "campus crazes"— panty raids, crowded Volkswagens and phone booths, anti-war riots, nude individuals "streaking" through public

places, and so forth. One "good story" breeds
another.

"Good stories" also are repeated on a regional
basis. Recently a fat man in London got a dentist to
wire his mouth shut so he could reduce despite a
weak will. It was a "good story" and papers all over
the world ran it. Then other fat people did it and
papers ran repeat stories as the fat people involved
got closer to home. Finally, for some papers, at least,
a fat person in the home town called to announce that
he was having his face wired. A reporter was sent out
to interview him and a story was run. Home town is
as close as you can get, so that was the end of that
particular "good story."

Another version of the unexpected is the story of
small (weak) overcoming big (strong). We've been
repeating that one in infinite variety since David
zonked Goliath.

Often we ignore quite legitimate needs in favor of
something bizarre or unusual or appealing. Take, for
instance, the case in August 1974 of the young house-
wife in Sarasota, Florida. Her husband worked for a
plastering firm. He came home one pay day with no
pay check. A construction firm had not paid her husband's employer, he told her, and the employer was
unable to pay her husband's wages. The young
woman, of course, felt that she had a legitimate
complaint. Her husband had earned money that she
needed and he was unable to get it. But who would
listen to her? She was like the logger trying to be
heard when his lifestyle was threatened by the Supreme Court Justice. No one cared.

But the young woman had something the logger
didn't, an attractive posterior. So she used it to get an
audience. She went to the sidewalk in front of the
construction company office, took her clothes off,
and picketed. She apparently notified the news

media first because there was a photographer on hand. She held her picket sign in front but there was nothing covering her posterior and the photographer got a shot from the rear. The young woman could not get a hearing for what she considered an important and legitimate complaint. Her attractive posterior had nothing to do with the complaint, of course, but she used what she had to gain attention.

I don't know whether her husband ever got paid or even what the local papers did with the story. But I know that the next day the picture of the young woman's bare backside arrived on the wirephoto machine in Everett, kitty-corner across the nation from Florida, and far from where anyone could help her husband get paid.

And that depicts a weakness of both the American social system and of American journalism. The social weakness is that it is difficult for little people, loggers and housewives, to make themselves heard regardless of their needs. The journalistic weakness is that we allow ourselves to be used by anyone who can invent a "good story," whether it is news or not.

Then, too, we allow ourselves to go to absurd lengths in our search for an "authority." We are taught in journalism school to go to a knowledgeable source for information, to go to a physician for information on bubonic plague, to ask an engineer for information on how a bridge should be built, to ask an economist about the cause of economic depressions, and so forth. That makes sense, of course, but often we let anyone who wants to become an expert. A man and his wife, for instance, may form the International Organization for World Peace. They elect him president and he makes announcements about methods for peace. If he is clever about it, he may land some of his views in the paper. Soon reporters begin calling him with questions about peace. The publicity attracts members to the club and eventually he becomes recognized as an authority on the subject simply because he is the president of an organization created by his own publicity.

If he is clever and lucky, no one will ever know that he is a major stockholder in a munitions factory. If he is caught, some reporter will be happy to break the story. But then, maybe he can move to another town, buy stock in the baby powder factory and become an authority on diaper rash.

That is why Mr. Kiersted complained during the Anacortes oil spill that "some reporters will print information without any verification at all, just because somebody said it."

Sometimes that practice is justified because the concept is such that it should be examined and discussed publicly regardless of the source. Sometimes, on the other hand, we use false authorities because we are too rushed—or too lazy—to find real ones. We may also use them because verification would interfere with a story that supports our prejudices or would ruin a "good story." In any case we defend ourselves on the basis that someone else said it.

All of these journalistic quirks and weaknesses can be and are used by propagandists with an axe to grind. The wilderness conservationists know that and have learned to take full advantage of it. They depend on prejudiced reporters to use advocacy journalism methods to emphasize their side and bury—or ignore—the other side. They use unprejudiced reporters' desire for a "good story" to plant stories to their liking. They tell, for instance, of calamities that will befall humanity if we upset ecology by not slavishly obeying their commands. They tell us that they are David fighting the Goliath of industry, government, or whatever adversary they have at the moment. They claim records of various kinds. They frighten us with stories of cancer epidemics if we do not obey them. They conduct nonnews programs such as young men walking and paddling around the world who pause occasionally to parrot the conservationists' story. They create instant experts by electing organization presidents, appointing committee chairmen, and granting other titles that imply knowledge. They also have on call various people of known prejudices whose credentials are real. Every wilderness conservation pressure group with any strength at all has available college professors, for instance, who can be depended on to testify predictably on almost any conservation-related subject.

They use social pressures and unrest such as the current distrust of the military-industrial complex and the instability of changing technology and changing institutions to plant ideas and to direct public response.

Propaganda has a snowball effect and affects reporters as much as readers. Once hoodwinked into publishing a misconception, a reporter is preconditioned to believe that misconception. If it was a "good story," he will be on the lookout for an opportunity to repeat it. And so will other reporters who read the first report.

An example of how propaganda slips into news media occurred as an aftermath of the tussock moth control program in the Pacific Northwest in 1974.

The tussock moth is endemic in Douglas fir forests such as those in the Pacific Northwest. Occasionally the moths break out in mass epidemics that damage vast areas of forests as they eat the fir needles.

Such an epidemic started in 1970. Ordinarily the epidemics last three years, then are controlled by natural enemies of the moth. The epidemic of the

1970s, however, was divided into several parts, each beginning in a different year so that the epidemic extended into five seasons instead of three.

At the time DDT was the only insecticide available to control the moth. The U. S. Environmental Protection Agency had outlawed the insecticide because of its residual effects on wildlife. The U. S. Forest Service in early 1973 asked for a special permit to use DDT on the tussock moth. Some 200,000 acres— billions of board feet—of forest were endangered. The service pledged to control the application so no permanent damage to wildlife or their environment would result.

Wilderness conservation organizations, of course, opposed the request. There were scientific studies and public hearings. The wilderness conservationists said 1973 was the third year and the tussock moth would die out naturally. The government scientists said there was more than one epidemic occurring consecutively and the moths would not all die out that year. EPA Director William Ruckelshaus heard the wilderness-conservationists rather than the government experts. He refused to issue the permit. The moth spread to the 200,000 acres as predicted.

In 1974 the Forest Service warned that 400,000 more acres were endangered and asked again for a permit. More scientific studies and public hearings. Incredibly, the wilderness conservationists repeated their argument about the three-year duration of tussock moth infestation.

Supporters of a control program pointed out that the epidemic already was in its fourth year. The Forest Service agreed that the epidemic probably would die out naturally the next season but not until after the 400,000 acres had been attacked. EPA had a new director, Russell Train. He made a face-saving attack on the Forest Service but granted the permit.

The wilderness conservation groups, of course, considered that an affront. They were incensed and they proclaimed their feelings loudly. DDT was used nevertheless. The forest was saved. Extensive studies by both federal and state scientific teams indicated danger to wildlife was minimal and temporary.

A few months later a Forest Service scientist, Dr. Robert Buckman, at a conference in Spokane said (as the Forest Service had repeated all along) that the tussock moth infestation would have died out naturally in 1974. That, he said, meant that if DDT had not been used in 1974 it would not have been necessary to use it in 1975. He did not clearly specify that the epidemic would not have died out naturally until after the moth had attacked the additional 400,000 acres of trees—in other words, that the use of DDT saved 400,000 acres of trees that would have been attacked before nature wiped out the moths. He did, however, state that the forest had been saved by the DDT.

UPI carried the story the next day. The article reported that Dr. Buckman pointed out that the infested timber stands might have been lost if the DDT had not been used. It gave, in general terms, both sides. The *Seattle Post Intelligencer* ran the story under a headline which said the moth was dying before the DDT spray program began. Quite true, as far as it went.

Two days later, the UPI ran an editorial under a headline which warned the reader not to fool with nature. The lead paragraph said the Forest Service that week had admitted that the use of DDT to kill the tussock moths "probably was unnecessary."[6] The editorial accused the Forest Service of having "down played" tussock moth population dynamics during the hearings and hinted that the Forest Service had

A small area of the 200,000 acres of Northwest forests attacked by tussock moths in 1973. The forests could have been saved by DDT but wilderness pressure groups prevented use of the insecticide even though scientists testified it could be used safely. Scientists' words later were twisted to give pressure groups a false propaganda victory.

stifled its own scientists and had ignored the evidence. The rest of the editorial was a repetition of the oft repeated warnings about DDT. It mentioned effects on "earth's life chain." It mentioned cancer. And it warned Americans not to lift the ban again.

In other words, a statement in Spokane on Tuesday by a man who believes the use of DDT on the tussock moth was both right and necessary was used in Seattle, three hundred miles away, three days later, as the foundation for an editorial 180 degrees opposed to what that man believed.

I do not think for a moment that whoever wrote that editorial deliberately lied. I believe that he saw only what he wanted to see in the UPI story and that he wrote the editorial in the conviction that evil forces in the Forest Service had finally exposed themselves and admitted the truth which he had known all along. He felt not only justified but duty bound to comment on what he believed to be the admission and to repeat the basically sound but grossly exaggerated charges against DDT. He may not know, even yet, that no such admission ever was made.

Good story, prejudice, weak versus strong, calamities, repeated stories, false authorities, epidemics, cancer—all are involved in this one case of what the pressure groups must consider a classic success in propaganda.

Propaganda has a way of spreading to the point of self-generation within nonparticipating agencies. An example is the public service spot announcements some radio stations have used to help the Forest Service justify its requirement that people obtain permits to enter wildernesses. The announcements unequivocally state that the permits are necessary to protect the environment of the wilderness. There is little justification for the claim but the stations air it and are given credit for performing a public service by the Federal Communications Commission.

But the most amusing secondary propaganda piece was a movie made some years ago by the U. S. Park Service—at public expense. It was meant to persuade people that they should stay out of the parks except for rare visits in which they enter only as backpackers. It treated all other kinds of park visitors with sarcasm and contempt. A most memorable sequence showed a chubby guy with a cigar in his mouth. Displayed nearby were water skis and a camper. He was shown saying that he was a citizen and a taxpayer and he felt entitled to use the parks. The sequence was supposed to be sarcasm. It failed. The chubby guy's statements rang true. Why shouldn't he have the use of the parks?

So the Park Service made additional footage of the movie—more taxpayer expense. The added footage, complete with dramatic music, explained that the first part really was sarcasm and that the maker of the movie did not actually believe the chubby guy should be allowed to water ski or have a camper in the National Park.

That made even less sense. The Park Service, as far as I have been able to find out, rarely shows the film to the public.

The failure of the Park Service movie was unusual. The wilderness-conservation propaganda nearly always is effective. That is true whether the propagandists are publishing books, using journalism's weaknesses to plant their arguments in the media, or working with secondary propaganda agencies. The result has been a mass overselling of the wilderness environmentalists' viewpoint. So much so that opposing views, however valid, are shut out. Like the invincibility of Pearl Harbor in 1941, the dogma of the wilderness conservationists has become unquestionable, accepted generally because they are generally accepted. It is when one side dominates that propaganda commits its crimes and that is what has happened in the wilderness-conservation movement.

CHAPTER FIVE

Living where I do, if I were to keep an eye on all the purely city governmental agencies that affect my life, I would have to attend the city council meetings every Tuesday, the planning commission meetings on the second and fourth Wednesdays of the month, the board of adjustment meetings on the third Wednesday, the park board meetings on the fourth Monday, the amenities design board on the first Wednesday, and the Civil Service Commission on the second Monday. That, of course, is to ignore the meetings of boards and commissions in neighboring cities where I have no voice but which still affect my life. There also are school, hospital, fire, and water districts, to say nothing of the county government and all its branches, the state, the federal government, and even international agencies. Even if I were to quit my job and devote full time to attending meetings, obviously I couldn't begin to keep up.

That is the key to the power of pressure groups. They attend for me. They persuade the officials that they speak for me and for all the public. They demand that their policies and goals be approved in my name and the names of all the other people who are not there. They may also make judicious use of money through campaign contributions or even outright bribes, but basically, their power lies in their ability to convince the decision makers that they are the voice of the people.

The success of any pressure group depends largely on how successful it is in putting across that deception. The wilderness conservation groups are masters of that deception, largely because they make adroit use of the techniques of propaganda and take advantage of the instability, insecurity, and public unrest caused by the rapid and interdependent changes in technology, politics, government, and social institutions.

They have been so clever in manipulation of those forces that they have persuaded much of officialdom that they speak for the people. That has given them tremendous, almost irresistible power. Unfortunately they are not the kind of people who can use such power either wisely or well.

The North Cascades National Park is an example of just how powerful they have become. The park and its adjacent recreation areas amount to about 700,000 acres of land that once was part of the old Mount Baker National Forest. In the 1950s the wilderness conservation groups demanded that a large part of the forest be declared wilderness and managed for their exclusive use.

The Forest Service was aware that the wilderness groups were becoming tremendously powerful, but it had not yet learned just how powerful. The service laid out a plan for establishing a wilderness in the area where the pressure groups had demanded it. But, aware that it had a duty to represent other interests, the service compromised. Its plan for wilderness did not include all the areas nor as many acres as the pressure groups had demanded. Much of the land was reserved for other types of recreation and for that other use hated by wilderness conservation groups, the logging that provides people with lumber for homes and paper for books.

The plan, made public in 1960, enraged wilderness conservation groups. They considered the compromise an affront, a challenge to their power, an insult to their egos. They vowed revenge and announced they would teach the Forest Service, a branch of the Agriculture Department, a lesson by taking the land away from that agency and giving it to the National Park Service, a branch of the Interior Department.

The enormity of the threat was self-evident. Many of us did not believe the pressure groups had the power to carry it out. Some of us scoffed. We were wrong. Before the decade was over, by 1968, Congress adopted legislation creating the park and the President signed it into law.[1]

The lesson was obvious to everyone involved. The bureaucracy in the Agriculture and Interior Departments both understood from the moment the North Cascades Park was formed that the wilderness-conservation groups had gathered enormous power that was extremely dangerous to resist. Nor was the lesson lost on other government agencies—federal, state, even local. Any agency involved in administering land knew from then on that crushing power lay in the hands of the pressure groups. It takes a brave bureaucrat, indeed, to stand up to that power, even when he knows it represents the true interests of only a small number of people.[2]

Nor was the lesson wasted on the pressure groups

themselves. I think they also were astonished by the magnitude of their success in the North Cascades. As a result the park, I believe, has become a symbol for them, a symbol of their power, a symbol on which their egos can feed voraciously and incessantly. For that reason they guard it jealously and sustain it tenderly. Congress, in creating the park, made a few minor compromises, leaving out relatively small pieces of land the wilderness-conservationists wanted. They have worked ever since to gain those areas. The pressure groups react strongly to any plans the Park Service puts forth to develop the park for people other than purist backpackers. They have opposed, for instance, plans to put in a tramway—see Chapter 4—and the Park Service proposal to establish hiker hostels in the back country met with furious objections. Most of all, they have fought Seattle City Light's plans to increase the electrical generating capacity of its Ross Dam in the Ross Lake Recreation Area.

Plainly the pressure groups consider the North Cascades, even more than other places, their private domain. The government and public interfere at their own risk.

The pressure groups exert their will partly through effective, sophisticated lobbies that operate smoothly and strongly in Washington, D. C., state capitals, and other seats of power. The wilderness conservation lobbies have become so powerful that even the large, well-heeled lobbies of the nation's business community find it difficult to oppose them effectively.

The ordinary individual simply is powerless.[3] When he tries to oppose the wilderness groups' lobby, he finds it difficult even to be heard, let alone to influence decisions. The individual always has the option, of course, of writing his congressman. But the wilderness conservation groups can, almost at a moment's notice, generate hundreds, sometimes thousands of letters on almost any given subject, for or against. They can do that through the organization leaders who have on hand lists of members brainwashed by internal propaganda. Many of those members will write whatever they are told to write simply because they are told to. The individual can't compete.

An even more rewarding field of battle for the pressure groups are the legislative and administrative public hearings. The wilderness conservationists have developed techniques for exerting tremendous influence on such hearings. The fact that they thereby prostitute meetings held for the express purpose of hearing all sides of a question seems to bother them not at all. Indeed, I suspect they revel in it.

The biggest single factor in their power to influence—and even control—what the investigators will hear during a public meeting is their ability to stack the hearings. In the same way that the membership responds on command to a call for letters, it will turn out for meetings and hearings. The leadership, thus, is able to use sheer numbers to outmaneuver and overwhelm the efforts of industry and of citizens interested in other recreational pursuits. The pressure groups simply call out so many members that all other voices are smothered.

They have developed a strategy that amounts almost to a formula. On the morning that the hearing is to begin, the floor leader takes a conspicuous place in the meeting room. He probably is a paid professional but occasionally one of the more prestigious members of the pressure groups' establishment takes over. His job is to orchestrate and direct the hearing strategy. The people taking part in the pressure groups' presentation look to him for instruction, encouragement and organization.

Sometimes the floor leader wears a badge of identification such as an arm band. The badge shows the troops where to look for instructions. To some degree it may be superfluous. In at least some cases the troops have met previously to receive instructions and to rehearse.

The troops consist of various types of people from middle-aged—or older—middle-class, well-to-do, to young children. They include the usual young dropouts who form an unnatural alliance with the largely middle-class wilderness movement because the movement opposes business and industry and industrial production.

Often many of the troops are college and high school students, recruited from the campus wilderness conservation organizations and environmental courses. The students are easy to get; they have time to attend the meetings. Sometimes a teacher is willing to recommend that his students attend, sometimes a teacher is willing to give extra credit to students who attend, but most of all, I imagine, students are more likely to be naive and impressionable and to do as they are told unquestioningly.

The purpose of the hearings invariably is to provide a forum for the decision makers to get all the information available on the subject at hand. It is not in the pressure groups' interest for the decision makers to hear both sides and they take steps to control what is said and how it is said.

A major part of the strategy is to intimidate the opposition. The method varies to some degree with how much control the hearing chairman exerts. But it always has the same primary purpose, to unnerve those who speak in opposition so they will make a poor impression. A secondary purpose is to encourage those who testify for the wilderness.

The methods are simple. They form a mass claque. They applaud friendly speakers; they boo and hiss unfriendly ones. They laugh sarcastically, *en masse*, when an unfriendly speaker makes a point. They shout insults and counterarguments while an unfriendly speaker is on the platform.

If the chairman maintains control and prohibits the more boisterous interruptions, they can achieve the same purpose by sighing at crucial points, by frowning at unfriendly speakers, by smiling at speakers on their side, by fidgeting in their chairs, by whispering to each other.

Once during a hearing on a proposed wilderness, a number of wilderness conservationists demanded that the wilderness be created. One result would be that people with four-wheel drive vehicles would be barred. There were a handful of members of a four-wheel drive club in the audience. One listened until he could stand it no longer. He jumped up and shouted something like, "If that's the way it is, maybe we should stop bringing our vehicles in to help rescue backpackers when they get hurt in the back country." The wilderness conservationists responded with cheers, whistles, foot stomping, applause instantly and thunderously. One man near me shouted, "That's what we want."

The response was completely irrational, of course. Even the purest wilderness conservationist doesn't want to be left injured in the mountains. But irrational or no, the demonstration was entirely successful. The four-wheel drive man sat down in confusion, defeated and silenced.

The outburst was spontaneous. There was no direction, no signal. The wilderness conservationists knew instinctively that a boisterous, irrational response would be most likely to silence their adversary's telling—though emotional—argument. Silencing their adversaries is a major goal of wilderness-conservationists.

Another time, I saw an old gentleman completely bewildered. To make a point in his plea for consideration of the need for manufacturing resources he asked a rhetorical question of the young people in the audience: "How many of you would like to be out of work when you have families to support?"

Every young person in the room held up his hand. The man was not experienced at public speaking. He was stumbling through his presentation anyway. It must have taken tremendous courage to get up before that audience. But he felt it was important to air his viewpoint and he made the attempt. The display of hands so completely confused him that his presentation fell to pieces.

The young people in that hearing room did not want to be unemployed. The speaker had simply given them an opening and spontaneously they thrust in their collective stiletto. Pressure groups don't like other views being aired.

People can be psyched out even before they begin their presentations. That sometimes happens to the business types at a conservation hearing. But, in a way, they ask for it. In the first place they are out of uniform and out of place. They always are vastly outnumbered and they wear conservative business suits where most of the others are in sports clothes or jeans. They sense the hostility of the crowd and often sit with other businessmen in a front row. They clutch their brief cases and speak only to each other in soft, nervous voices. They stand out like chickens in the fox's den. And they get about the same treatment.

Their adversaries simply glare them down. They

glare at them from behind, from in front, from the side. They glare at them straight on. They glare at them from the corners of their eyes. They glare at them before the hearing begins. They glare at them while it's going on. They glare at them as they prepare to make their presentation. They glare at them as they make their presentation. Always with the same hostile, contemptuous expression.

The businessmen usually are highly placed individuals in their corporations. They are used to being treated with respect, even deference. I imagine they are aware that some of the people who work for them are secretly hostile but they are not used to open hostility.

Some are able to bear up under the strain. Some are not. I've seen some pretty tough captains of industry break under it, and blow their presentations. That, of course, is greeted with catcalls and laughter, and they lose their composure even more.

If unnerving the opposition is one goal at a hearing, another is to parade large numbers of people before the investigators. The opposition usually consists of a few businessmen, perhaps some backpackers interested in limiting the regimentation that is a necessary adjunct of declaring wilderness areas. There probably also will be a few people interested in using the land for some recreational pursuit other than backpacking—motorcyclists, horse riders, campers, rock hounds, amateur prospectors, skiers, four-wheel-drive people, and so forth. If they are organized at all, it is likely to be loosely. So they are not able to get as many people to the meeting as the wilderness-conservationists. Nor are they able to orchestrate their presentations as well. They are soon finished, leaving the field entirely to the wilderness-conservationists.

And the wilderness-conservationists take full

advantage. They parade people before the investigators sometimes literally for days on end.

Who the speakers are or what they say makes little difference. Recently, at the Ross Dam hearings in Seattle, the administrative judge, Allen Lunde, during the third or fourth day of endless and usually meaningless testimony suddenly blurted in exasperation, "All I'm hearing is generalities and clichés." He was right. And he had several more days of it coming. The pressure groups' objective is to get large numbers of witnesses. What they say is unimportant.

I've heard, for instance, a hippie contend that people should be limited to a single light bulb in their homes to reduce electrical consumption. I've heard a young man make an impassioned plea for saving the grizzly bears and wolves in country where grizzly bears and wolves never had existed. I've heard a man say he believed the people of New York would gladly sacrifice their supply of toilet paper if they felt that would ensure wilderness classification for more forests in Washington. I've heard a man testify that trails could not be built where they obviously could be. I've heard the president of the University of Washington Gay Liberation Club demand wilderness classification for a mountain area because his club liked to take hikes there.[4]

Large numbers of speakers and a demonstrative, sympathetic audience are the major goals of pressure groups out to stack a public hearing. But the orchestration also extends to the types of people who parade to the stand. The more appealing, the better. The purpose is to evoke sympathy for the cause through the image projected by the speakers. Who they are and what they say are unimportant. The important thing is that they are appealing. The choice almost certainly will include a major proportion of pretty young women. A child will be put on the rostrum to talk about being denied his heritage. He may also say in childlike innocence that he can't understand why anyone would want to "destroy" (a key word in the wilderness-conservation propaganda lexicon) a beautiful place like that (whatever place happens to be the topic of the hearing). The child may be followed by an old man who has to be helped to the stand and who stumbles piteously over his lines as he says he has been hiking in that country for 60 years and he thinks it should be "preserved" (another key word) for future generations.

Some PhDs and college professors whose viewpoints coincide with that of the wilderness conservation establishment are likely to be dug up. The learned ones lend dignity to the cause and nullify the testimony of expert witnesses on the other side.

The pressure groups delight in having speakers that evoke sympathy or credibility but the main emphasis is on numbers, regardless of what they say and of who they are. The name of the game is to get out many times more people than the opposition and to pretend that the general population is on their side. Several hundred single-minded persons organized to attend a public hearing do not speak for 220 million Americans, but the object is to make it seem that they do.

The pressure groups' leaders have four major goals for the careful and precise programming of public hearings. The most obvious, of course, is to impress the agency conducting the hearing—be it a congressional committee or a branch of the administration—with their political strength. Their rational arguments could be presented in a few minutes of factual presentation. And indeed they take care to see that the record contains all their valid points in a clear and concise way. But their parade of speakers saying the same thing over and over again for hours—or days—on end gets into the record the unmistakable message that regardless of facts and reason public officials had better take note that the wilderness-conservationists control people who are both organized and disciplined.

Another reason for stacking the public hearings is the effect on the audience. The show of solidarity and organization has a discernible strengthening effect on the morale and emotions of the faithful. At the same time it tends to destroy the morale of the opposition. The psychology of the pressure group membership at the public hearings is much like that of a lynch mob. Each individual affects and is affected by all the others until the group takes on a character of its own and the rightness of the group and its goals become unquestionable.

A third reason for the presentations is to set the stage for court action. A favorite tactic of the wilderness-conservationists has been to use court injunctions to temporarily tie up public land for their own purposes and to prevent programs they don't like. Armed with vast funds from the dues and donations of the membership, they can afford to go to court through long trials and appeals on many matters. Win, lose, or draw, they tie the hands of public administrators through the proceedings which may take many years. Corporations and governmental agencies, of course, can meet them in court on a more or less equal basis. The ordinary citizen, however, stands no chance. No matter how strongly he may feel on a subject, there is little opportunity unless he is wealthy for him to have a day in court. He simply can't afford it. He can only watch helplessly.

The fourth, but not least, reason for stacking the public hearings is the effect on the news media. The period before the hearing is likely to see newsrooms warned by the pressure groups that they intend to create controversy at the hearing. Since we love contention, that brings large numbers of reporters to the hearing room.[5] Many of the reporters are assigned because they are interested in the environmental or wilderness movements which usually means they are sympathetic to those movements. The others are looking for a "good story" and the odds are long that the wilderness-conservationists' orchestration will make their side a "good story."

And, an important part of the "good story" is likely to be the large number of prowilderness people who parade to the speakers' stand. The pressure group leadership will be careful to plant the idea that theirs is the side of the people, the weak and the oppressed—David—while the opposition is huge, evil, and greedy corporations, government agencies or, best, both—Goliath.

In the beginning the pressure groups actually were small and weak. But, like David, once they had slain the giant they went on to become the rich and all-powerful king able to confront enemies with over-whelming strength and to ignore the rights of common citizens. Wilderness-conservation pressure groups, however, are expert at projecting the image that they are small and weak. In doing so they provide a "good story" that many reporters will center on. Thus the next day the media's readers, viewers and listeners are likely to read, see, and hear that there were scores of speakers for the wilderness and only a handful against. The less observant and more prejudiced reporters will go the whole way and present the prowilderness speakers as representing the people and the antiwilderness speakers as "commercial interests." They do that even though it should be obvious to all present that most of the antiwilderness speakers are people with no commercial interest whatsoever but are individuals who know that if the land is declared wilderness they will be denied its use for recreation.[6]

Not all of the stories will be thus twisted, of course. But many will and that will be another propaganda victory for the pressure groups. And to compound the victory the newspapers almost certainly will get letters to the editors in large number saying something like the "testimony was more than four to one for wilderness, ample proof that the people overwhelmingly favor it."

The control of public hearings plus the immense propaganda programs of the pressure groups have a serious effect on many of the men and women who work for the public agencies involved. Because they hear so much of the wilderness-conservation arguments and so little from the others, some come to believe that they do the people's will when they accept the dictates of the pressure groups. Sometimes they become so thoroughly convinced of the infallibility of the wilderness groups that they attempt to pressure their colleagues to agree. To illustrate, let me tell you about two Forest Service rangers:

On a recent Labor Day weekend my daughter, Meri, and I climbed Three Fingers Mountain with Harold Engles. The peak is only eight miles from the road but we got a late start. A mile or so short of the peak the trail was still covered with the previous winter's snow and dusk was approaching so we decided to camp there. The next morning, Harold showed us how to avoid the dangerous, snow-covered portions of the trail by going over a glacier, around some crevasses, and up a rock chimney. Then we went over a snow field and up the rock peak to where a ladder leads to the abandoned fire lookout on the top.

At first he held back so Meri and I could keep up. But Harold loves the mountains and he loves climbing and the nearer we got to the top the harder it was for him to hold back. Soon he was far out in front of us. When we finally reached the peak, he was fresh and ready as a puppy at dinnertime. Amazing. It was his seventy-second birthday.

In 1929 Forest Ranger Harold Engles and his friend Harry Bedal were the first two men to climb Mount Three Fingers. Here he pauses on a glacier near the top when he revisited the peak forty-five years later.

Harold and I had been talking about a climb of Three Fingers for months. I was especially anxious to go with him because I wanted to do a story on the mountain. Harold and the late Harry Bedal, another mountain professional, had been the first men to climb it. And they had been the bosses of the crew that built the lookout cabin. Harold has climbed the mountain many times. He knows it well.

The first climb was in 1929 when Harold was about twenty-seven. Harold had gone to work for the Forest Service when he was sixteen. He took some time out to go to forestry school at college and in 1926 he was appointed ranger of the Darrington District.

He married a Darrington girl and put his roots down in the little community deep in the Cascades. He was transferred for a time to a national forest in Oregon, but he wangled an assignment back in Darrington and except for occasional trips, never left the community again. As ranger he was responsible for hundreds of thousands of acres of forests and mountains. He and his crews protected the forests, fought fires in them, supervised logging in them, replanted them. Harold came to know that part of the country like he knew his own kitchen. He has climbed most of the peaks and he built most of the trails. He loves it all.

During his career as ranger in Darrington, Harold gained a reputation for feats of strength and endurance that still are talked about with awe by tough foresters. He could out-hike, out-work, and out-think most men in the forest and the stories about him are legion. The story I like best is the one about the logging operator whose carelessness caused a forest fire. While it was being fought, Harold said the operator would be charged the cost of fighting the fire.

The infuriated operator sent to Seattle and brought in a professional boxer. He gave the boxer $25 to teach Harold a lesson. When the boxer arrived at the fire camp, Harold was at the supply base several miles down the mountain. The operator and the boxer settled down to wait for him.

Harold, not knowing about the boxer, had gone to the supply camp to get a special pump that was needed at the fire line. The pump weighed 160 pounds and was designed to be broken down and carried by mules. There were no mules available so Harold rigged up a special pack, put the pump on his back, and went up the mountain.

Harold arrived in the fire camp carrying the pump. It took two men to lift it off his back and set it on the ground. Then Harold, without pausing to rest, went off to work on the fire line. The boxer watched all that, walked up to the operator, gave him back the $25, and hiked down the trail heading toward Seattle.

In addition to being tough and smart, Harold also is one of the best storytellers I've ever known. He has a personality that attracts people to him wherever he goes. His rich humor and his ability to string his stories together in a fascinating way bring hours of enjoyment just listening. I've seen him entertain for half an hour a dozen people he chanced to meet on the trail. He is a tremendous person and I consider it a privilege to know him. And I regret what happened to him.

Harold's philosophy demands that a man must do what he believes is right. If he is part of an organization that acts contrary to his conscience he has no honorable alternative but to get out.

Harold believes strongly that the national forests are the people's land, that they belong to all the people, and that they must be managed for the benefit of all the people. That means, in part, that the resources, the wood and metals of the forests, should be harvested for the people's economic welfare. It also means that at the same time the land should be managed so people interested in noncommercial pursuits may use and enjoy it as much as possible and with a minimum of interference from the government.

The philosophy of the Forest Service in Harold's day was to manage the land under what eventually become known as the "multiple use" concept. The slogan was "Land of many uses." The service listed those uses as wood, water, forage (for livestock), wildlife, and recreation.

The wilderness pressure groups, when they came on the scene, accepted recreation in part, but they redefined that concept to fit their own goals. Wildlife they accepted as reinforcing their recreation goals.[7] The same with water. Wood and forage they rejected out of hand.

By the 1950s the pressure groups were making their muscle felt. Increasingly the Forest Service's policies and programs were twisted and bent to favor the narrow goals of wilderness-conservationists. More and more, the Forest Service listened to the tiny minority of the wilderness-conservation movement. More and more, it compromised the multiple-use concept that served the nation and its people, all its people. More and more, Harold Engles found himself under orders to do things he felt did not well serve the people. "There's enough land here for everybody," Harold once told me. "It's wrong to lock it up for a favored few."

Harold is too much of a gentleman to censure or find fault. He never in my presence has criticized the superiors who gave him the orders he felt were wrong. Once, I asked him about it directly. He simply said, "They were under pressures they couldn't resist. They had no choice. I don't blame them." But blame or no, it got to the point where Harold felt he no longer could honorably be involved. He took early retirement from the Forest Service, left the career he loved.

Harold has a small farm in Darrington where he raises much of what he uses. His partial pension is sufficient, though not large. He and Mrs. Engles are, I'm sure, comfortable. But Harold, even yet, is hurt and disappointed by what happened. He doesn't complain but you can see it in his expression when you ask him about it. And in the quick way he changes the subject.

The other ranger I'd like to tell about is Cal Dunnell. I disagree with Cal and we argue a lot but Cal is a man of integrity and honor. He says what he says and does what he does because he believes in it. He is a wilderness-conservationist, but a crusader, not a profit seeker or a pressure reliever.

The first time I met Cal was when he led a party of reporters and cameramen on a press trip to Image Lake in the Glacier Peak Wilderness. There must have been a dozen or so people from newspapers, magazines, radio, and TV. And perhaps half that many Forest Service people. Part of their job was to get us up the twelve-mile trail so we could see what was there. The rest of their responsibility was to get us back to civilization without injury or heart attack. I think they realized the scope of the job when one of the TV reporters showed up carrying a suitcase.

Cal is short but he is wide in the shoulders and tremendously powerful. Like Harold Engles, he loves the forests and mountains, loves to work in them and be in them.

He also likes animals, including, I think, horses. But even if he likes horses, he doesn't like to ride them. The press trip to Image Lake was a horse trip but Cal declined to get on one. He helped saddle them, feed them, corral them, and herd them. But when we

Forest Service horsemen lead a press party to Image Lake in
Glacier Peak Wilderness.

were on the trail he walked, leading his horse by the reins.

I got to know Cal pretty well on that trip. It didn't take long to learn he had a different viewpoint from mine but that isn't really important. The other things I noticed were that he could spend the whole day herding that mess of reporters and animals up the hill, then take care of the horses, show the neophytes how to take care of themselves, cook the dinner, and carry on an educational program. He did all of that casually, easily, and with an even temper, although I knew he must be dead tired and exasperated with the ignorance of some of his charges.

I've seen Cal many times since then. In his office, on the street, at public meetings, and in the mountains. I've come to know him well.

I suspect that when he was a young man, he must have agreed with Harold Engle's viewpoint, and mine, that multiple use meant that the land managed by the Forest Service should be retained for all of the people. But gradually, I think, the pressures of the times and the wilderness conservationists got to him and he became convinced that he was doing the public's work by taking increasing steps to "protect" the land, restricting the right of people to use it, to visit it, to see it, to enjoy it.

Cal kept talking about the Forest Service having a "moral duty" to prevent the "rape" of the mountains by people. He often repeated the wilderness-conservation propaganda slogan about people "loving to death" the forests and mountains.

Cal was the recreation assistant to the supervisor of the Mount Baker National Forest when I was covering that forest for the *Herald*. Every time I saw him he seemed to have a new plan for keeping people out of the forest "to protect it." Or for restricting, regimenting them while they were in it. He was convinced the mountains were "fragile" and were being "destroyed" and if that happened, it would be his fault.

We argued a lot. I used to tell him the mountains were there before man came and they would be there after man was gone. He was, I insisted, overreacting and I teased him about putting up signs that said "This is Your National Forest. Keep Out." Why not, I would ask, establish protective facilities in the more popular places and just let people alone to enjoy themselves in the other places?

"They'll damage the environment," Cal would say.

"What damage?" I would respond. "So they wear some trails and flatten some camping areas. So what? That's a few acres out of hundreds of thousands. And the damage isn't all that important, anyway."

"The people expect us to prevent that," Cal would say.

"Not the people, the pressure groups. That's not the same thing."

"The letters and comments we get are ten to one in favor of protection."

"Those are form lett,rs, caused by the organizations. They represent only a small fraction of the people."

And so our conversations went. Sometimes for hours on end.

Before I knew him Cal was the ranger of the forest's Skagit District. He instituted the rebuilding of the trail to Cascade Pass. The pass is on the crest of the Cascades. The trail is only about four miles long, gentle and easy. After it was rebuilt it became possibly the most popular trail in the range. It was so gentle and easy and the pass was so beautiful that tens of thousands of people hiked it. Many were people who would never make another venture into the mountains, people from the cities and farms of the entire nation.

The people wore some of the vegetation from the top of the pass. They wore side trails to the high spots and the vegetation was damaged in a few places that were popular for resting, lunch eating, or camping. Those spots were neither widespread nor important. The pass was still an immensely beautiful place. The bare spots, if they had any effect at all, simply emphasized and enhanced the beauty of the view, providing contrast and form to the expanses of green growth and grey rock.

Wilderness-conservationists, of course, would have none of that. They complained that it had become an "ecological disaster area." They denounced what they called the "destruction" of the "fragile environment." They further denounced the Forest Service official who had built the new trail—Cal.

"Rebuilding the trail to Cascade Pass was the worst mistake I ever made," Cal once told me.

"What mistake, Cal?" I asked. "You made it possible for tens of thousands of people to see that utterly beautiful country. It isn't really much of a hike but many of those thousands are city people from the East. That one hike is the only time they will get into the back country during their entire lives. It is an experience they will remember and love. It is an education that will profit them beyond anything they can get from books. The new trail is an immense service to the country. How can you think it was a mistake?"

When the Mount Baker Forest was absorbed by the Snoqualmie, Cal was transferred to the Wenatchee National Forest on the other side of the Cascades. I shook hands and said goodby sadly, because I knew I would miss Cal and our long-standing arguments. I enjoyed talking to him even though I doubted he would ever be converted.

But now I'm not so sure. One recent summer the news desk sent me over to the Wenatchee Forest to cover a forest fire. At the base camp, I ran into Cal who was in charge of the supply tent. We chatted for a while. I tried to bait him into resuming our argument. No luck. In fact, he told me he had been up to inspect a place adjacent to the Alpine Lakes Area that the pressure groups were demanding be included in the new wilderness that was being created there. "I can't see why they want that flat land," Cal said. "I just can't see what they're talking about."

Coming from Cal, that was a tremendous admission. I think it was a turning point for me. Until then I had thought that the pressure groups were simply too powerful. So powerful that it was a waste of time to oppose them.

But if Cal could begin to wonder about them, maybe it would be possible to defeat them. I don't know. Maybe that was when I decided it might not be entirely foolhardy to write a book asking that the people's land be given back to the people.

I don't mean to imply that Cal has had some sort of miraculous conversion, that he has reversed himself and become anti wilderness. He hasn't and he won't. The point is that he has learned to question. He had been buffeted by the pressures and propaganda of the wilderness groups until, like many others, he came to accept their dictates unquestioningly. But that was only temporary. Eventually I think he began to see through their excesses and distortions and he learned to question. He is not anti wilderness. Nor am I. We both believe in wilderness but wilderness limited in area. And wilderness limited in the restrictions imposed on the people who use it.

Cal, I'm sure, will accept larger wilderness areas and more severe restrictions than I would like, but that's all right. We both are willing to consider each other's position, to work toward managing the public lands so they best serve the most people. Cal, to my mind, is still a wilderness conservationist but not the fanatic kind, the kind who demands ever more wilderness, ever more tightly regulated. I have no criticism with Cal's kind of wilderness conservationism. My quarrel is with the fanatics and this book is about them.

Who are they? The answer to that is not as simple as it might seem. One trouble is that everyone is pro wilderness. I don't know anyone who isn't a conservationist. I've never met anyone who isn't concerned about the ecology. The difference is a matter of degree and it is difficult to say exactly where is the line between reason and unreason.

But the wilderness-conservationists I'm writing about go beyond that line wherever it is. Maybe what they do is use the fact that people are concerned about the environment, use that to further their own causes. And, perhaps those causes don't always involve wilderness, conservation, the environment, or anything connected with them.

It may not be possible to precisely identify the wilderness-conservationist I'm writing about but there are some generalizations to be made.

It is nothing new to say they are a greed-ridden elite. That has been said many times. Apparently it stings. They go to great lengths to deny it.

It is true, nevertheless, of most of the people this book concerns. They are usually the well-to-do who have solved their most pressing personal economic problems and feel no compulsion to help solve anyone else's. They see nothing wrong with gaining private recreation grounds at the cost of depriving people in need of the product of millions of acres of land. They see nothing wrong with excluding people with other recreational interests from that same land.

The wilderness-conservationists this book opposes

are probably members or officers of one or more of the more militant, uncompromising, close-minded environmental organizations such as but not limited to the Sierra Club, the Wilderness Society and Friends of the Earth.

They are usually well-educated professional and semiprofessional people who well know the workings of government and the means for influencing it. Sometimes they are the drop-outs whose goal often is to punish (or destroy) society for being society.

They usually are to some degree outdoorsmen but on an amateur basis. They see outdoors as primarily a recreation area, not as a work area or a production area. They seldom can match the professional in skill or knowledge about the outdoors but they know how to control the decision-making apparatus so the voice of the professional is muted.

They form a clique, an establishment, an in group, a mutual admiration society whose first requirement of membership is unquestioning acceptance of the credo. Members must also accept uncritically the dogma that the clique is made up entirely of superior people. Each individual thus feeds and at the same time feeds on the egos of all the others.

They share an ability to reject or shut out external ideas.

They often are ruthless, even vicious, and are convinced that the end justifies the means.

Their actions are single-minded. They present questions and programs in either-or language. They seldom recognize trade-offs. They brook no compromise. They recognize no alternatives. They demand their goals in entirety. They condemn all other goals and the people who propose them.

Many, but not all, are profit seekers or pressure relievers. The profit seekers use the crusade to further their own interests, to provide themselves with jobs or professional aggrandizement or business opportunities. The pressure relievers use it to relieve their internal pressures. Some have psychological needs to harm people such as government officials who can be attacked with impunity. They attack commercial interests that can be vilified safely because business is suspect in today's society. They take part in the battle not because they care about the goals but because it gives them a platform from which they may attack people without fear of being hurt themselves.

They are, in short, people whose internal pressures drive them to strike out as a safety valve. They need such a release to prevent them from becoming violent under the strain. They need help and they can find it no other way. Pressure relievers, like profit seekers, are to be feared by society and individuals. But, unlike the profit seekers, they are to be pitied.

An alternative motivation for profit seekers and pressure relievers is simply the accumulation of personal power. The ability to influence or dictate society's decisions is sufficient goal in itself for some pressure relievers and an avenue to wealth for some profit seekers.

This book also concerns wilderness-conservationists who are not profit seekers or pressure relievers but are the mindless, thoughtless type of crusaders who accept blindly the dictates of the profit seekers and pressure relievers. They are honestly concerned and they are convinced that theirs is the right course. But their concern and conviction are based on the words of false leaders whom they follow blindly. They consider no other values. They are people who write letters, sign petitions, and make statements simply because they are told to. They are, unwittingly, the individuals who give the profit seekers and pressure relievers the power to steal the people's land.

But they are not the crusaders who approach the problem with intellectual honesty, like the Seattle Mountaineers and individuals like Cal Dunnell who are trying to find the right way to do what is necessary, who want to serve society and are trying to find how best to do it. Crusaders with an open mind are both desirable and necessary whether the contention is over wilderness or any other value. And whether they agree with me or not. The end does not justify the means for that kind of crusader.

CHAPTER SIX

Wilderness as we know it now in this country was established—and created—by the Wilderness Act of 1964.

The senate version was written by Senator Henry M. Jackson. In the House, Representative Lloyd Meeds has been a staunch supporter of the philosophy expressed by the act. It is no accident that both of those men are from Everett. Nor is it an accident that this book is written by a reporter from Everett.

The Wilderness Act is largely a product of our part of the country and is of particular concern to its people. The mountains of Washington are an important influence on the lives of everyone in the state, even those who rarely visit them and know almost nothing about them.

The mountains, for instance, make our weather. The wet Pacific Ocean winds drop their moisture as they rise over the Olympic and Cascade Ranges. By the time they get to the east side of the Cascades they are dry. The west side of the range, thus, is wet and rainy with dense forests. A few miles away, on the east side, the forests support different species of trees, widely spaced. The air becomes dryer as it travels further east until by midstate the land is arid, desertlike, basking under a nearly constant sun.

The mountains are a cultural barrier and always have been. Before white men came, the Indians on the east side were nomadic, relatively poor, prairie people. The west side people had permanent wooden houses and an abundance of wealth, so much wealth that they had leisure to develop fairly sophisticated arts and crafts. Now the east side is largely agricultural while the west side is industrial.

Even today there are only six highways across the Cascades in the 300 mile width of the state.

The mountains influence our economics and our politics. The rural east side usually votes Republican. The urban west side usually goes Democratic. For many of Washington's people the mountains are a work place. For others they are a playground. For some they are both.

It is difficult for people in other parts of the country to perceive how important the mountains are to us who live in their shadow. Since I grew up in Chicago and New York, I understand that difficulty. And, why shouldn't it be difficult for outsiders to know how the mountains affect their people. Even some of their people don't understand.

And to many of the people who don't understand, the Wilderness Act seemed like a savior of the traditions of the nation. It would preserve forever the free, unchanged, natural lands that were at the same time the cause and effect of the American dream, the American reality, and the American culture. To a

large extent that is true. The Wilderness Act is a good
law, a necessary one. The trouble is that it goes both
too far and not far enough.

The Wilderness Act attempts to freeze land, to
make it unchanging and unchanged, and to prevent
man from affecting it in any way. The Wilderness, in
the language of the act itself, is "an area where the
earth and its community of life are untrammeled by
man, where man himself is a visitor who does not
remain." The act also states that "Wilderness is
further defined to mean an area of undeveloped
Federal land retaining its primeval character and
influence, without permanent improvements or
human habitation, which is protected and managed
so as to preserve its natural conditions...." The law
also requires that the wilderness land must appear
"to have been affected primarily by the forces of
nature," provide "outstanding opportunities for soli-
tude or a primitive and unconfined type of recreation," and so forth.

All of that is wonderful, of course. It brings to mind
the American heritage of fresh, free, new land and the
brave frontiersmen who ventured into it alone and
independent. That picture isn't really true in today's
wilderness. An example of the misconception is the
story of the prospector in Horseshoe Basin near
Cascade Pass in what is now the North Cascades
National Park. One fall about the turn of the century
he broke his leg after his companions had left for the
winter. The young pioneer knew it would be impossible to survive the bitter cold and storms of winter
in Horseshoe Basin so he tried to crawl the thirty
miles to Stehekin, the nearest outpost of civilization.
He got eight miles to Bridge Creek. Some of his
friends found his frozen body there the next spring
and buried it where they found it. A friend of mine, a
long-time resident of Stehekin, says he thinks he

knows where that grave is. I hope to try to find it someday. I think it should be preserved as a memory of the past.

But that past is gone. Recently I accompanied rangers from the Stehekin office of the North Cascades National Park on a crosscountry ski trip up the Stehekin Valley to Bridge Creek. We stayed overnight in a cabin which must be somewhere near the grave. A major purpose of the trip was to look for persons who might have ventured too far into the valley and gotten into trouble. If the rangers had found someone or had had a report of someone missing, they had at their disposal the resources of the park plus scores of men and tons of equipment of the volunteer search and rescue units that operate throughout the Cascades.

The prospector with a broken leg might well have been rescued today. At any rate he would have had the knowledge that a major effort would be mounted to find him and bring him out.

But instead, he was fully aware that he was completely on his own. He would live or die solely on the basis of his own ability to solve his problems. Surely, even though he made a superhuman effort he knew that his problem could not be solved alone. That knowledge marked the essential difference between his real wilderness and the make-believe, wilderness-by-law of today.

The cold, hard fact is that the wilderness that prospector knew cannot be preserved or duplicated by law or by any other institution of civilization. The essential ingredient of that kind of pure wilderness is lack of civilization. It has long since disappeared. Any attempt to renew it by law only further deteriorates it because law and civilization are inseparable.

Law is the antithesis of wilderness.

Such wilderness-by-fiat, however, is not undesirable. It serves a real purpose, reminding us of the land and the self-sufficient, brave, capable people who made us what we are. There is a psychological value simply in knowing that there still is such land in the country, even though its people and the conditions that made them are irretrievably gone.

The question is, how much such land is necessary to fulfill those goals?

The answer is, not much.

The comment is, not much is needed for those purposes but we urgently need land for other purposes, both economic and recreational.

Land is the producer of the raw materials that humanity needs to sustain itself. The Cascades, for instance, contain some metals that could be added to the world's supply of useable material.[1] But most of the Cascades' resources are in the form of wood.

Forests, once harvested, renew themselves, regrow. Unharvested, they die naturally and eventually burn before they regrow. Even though there are psychological values to land left untouched, there is a limit to how much that kind of waste can be justified on those grounds. People need houses and paper and plastics. Those needs are more important than the psychological need of wilderness. It is important to find a logical balance.

Wilderness-by-fiat also has a serious effect on the possibilities for recreation in the outdoors, even for those of us who are primarily interested in backpacking, getting away from civilization with no more than we can carry on our backs. The fact is that there really are two kinds of wilderness. The Wilderness Act of 1964 preserves one at the expense of the other.

The first kind of wilderness, the one preserved by the law, is that of the land, the one described by the act as "earth...untrammeled by man." The other is the spiritual wilderness. It is achieved by getting away from civilization and its restrictions. The prospector whose grave I hope to find some day knew this kind of freedom as did Lewis and Clark and hoards of other pioneers who went into the wild lands and became completely self-sufficient. They were laws unto themselves, unprotected but uncontrolled, unconfined by other men, away from the rules, regulations, regimentation of civilization. Free.

Both kinds of wilderness cannot exist in the same place in today's world. The only way land can be "untrammeled by man" is to severely limit man's presence; and, when he is present, to severely limit what he does, how he does it, and where he goes. That, of necessity, means laws, rules, regulations, regimentation, and law enforcement officers. Land wilderness, obviously, destroys spiritual wilderness. The Wilderness Act protects the land wilderness, destroys the spiritual wilderness. Both are desirable, but there is a reasonable limit to how much land wilderness should be created at the expense of the spiritual wilderness. The Wilderness Act does not establish that limitation.

The wilderness conservationist organizations, run largely by profit seekers and pressure relievers, have long since lost the ability to control themselves. Their primary purpose no longer is to serve humanity. Their goal now is to provide profits and psychological relief to those leaders and members who are profit seekers and pressure relievers. The means to do that is to continue to take more and more land, to feed the egos and treasuries, to provide grist for the propaganda mills and to demonstrate the power of the group— the ultimate work of pressure groups.

What, for instance, would Lewis and Clark have thought if they had been met on the trail by a wilderness ranger who demanded to see their wilderness permit? That, of course, is just one of the nonwilderness, wilderness regulations they might encounter if they entered the wilderness today.[2]

Actually the wilderness permit system has been vastly overdone by the bureaucracies charged with maintaining the wilderness in an "untrammeled" condition. The bureaucracies involved are the National Park Service and the U. S. Forest Service. Even though Congress has ignored requests to formally designate most of the park land as wilderness, the Park Service requires permits of anyone who enters any of its back country for an overnight visit. The Forest Service requires permits in many of their wilderness areas, and there are indications it will extend the requirement to the other areas.

The Forest Service has offered a succession of reasons for the permits. Shortly after the Wilderness Act was passed, the service announced that the permits would give rangers an opportunity to talk to hikers, to direct them to the best places, and to instruct them on how to, as they put it, "protect the fragile environment" in the wilderness. The problem was that the permits almost always were issued by clerks in the ranger station. Usually the clerks gave a memorized spiel by rote. Only rarely were they able to answer even the most simple questions. Only rarely had they ever been to the wilderness themselves. They obviously did little to educate anyone about anything. The most preposterous aspect of the educational process was that the hiker got the same spiel each time he entered the wilderness. If he got 20 permits in a season, he heard the lesson twenty times. By season's end he might know it better than the series of clerks he heard it from, meaningless as it was.

The argument that permits were necessary to provide an educational opportunity flopped so the Forest Service changed. It began explaining that the permits provided information on who was in the wilderness and where so it would be easier to find people who got lost. The wildernesses, however, were only a relatively small part of Forest Service land; why wasn't the service concerned about people who got lost in nonwilderness areas? And wouldn't it be easier and cheaper to just put registration sheets at trailheads so people who wanted to be checked on could sign in. Besides, some persons who got a permit did not take the trip. Indeed, I have known people to get three permits for the same weekend because they weren't sure exactly where they wanted to go. If Forest Service people had followed up with searches for those persons who didn't go where they were supposed to, the rangers would have been busy. But they didn't.

So the service changed the story to say the permits were necessary so they could direct people away from those "fragile" areas that were being overused to areas that were relatively unused. That reason was obviously invalid since they required the same permit for the unused places as for the overused ones. It takes no great mentality to understand that if the service required permits for the popular places but not for the seldom visited places, the traffic in the popular places would diminish considerably. But the Forest Service completely overlooks that strategy. Indeed, when the Alpine Lakes Wilderness was created in 1976, the Forest Service announced it intended to require permits in the entire 400,000 acres, including the Enchantment Lakes area. Service officials admitted the bare, glaciated rock of the lakes could not be affected by any number of visitors but they said the permits were to be required "to keep too many people from going up there."

I have it on the authority of Forest Service people that there are less than 100 acres of "overused" land in all the wildernesses in Washington. Yet the Forest Service requires permits in more than one million acres of wilderness in that state. The overkill is undeniable.

So the Forest Service has come up with still

U.S. Forest Service admitted the glaciated rock surface of the Enchantment Lakes area could not be harmed by any number of visitors but announced it would require permits of visitors "to keep too many people from going up there."

another explanation (the current one at this writing). Now they say that the information they get from the permit copies is computerized so they can tell which areas get the most use, which trails need to be worked on, which campsites should be checked.

The young assistant ranger who first gave me that explanation is a recent forestry school graduate. He

seems wholly dedicated to wilderness, forests, and
the Forest Service—a likeable and intelligent young
man.

"Wouldn't it be easier to just go up and look at
those areas to see if they need work?" I asked. "Don't
you have to go up and look, anyway, to check on
what the computer tells you?"

"Yes," he said. He stared at me for a moment and
said, "They explained the need for the computer to us
but I didn't really understand. Neither did the others
at the meeting whom I asked. I guess you'll have to go
to somebody higher up for the real reason."

Later I talked to another man, much higher in the
Forest Service. He told me computerizing information taken from the permits is not worth the
expense. "We do it," he said, "because a majority of
people at a meeting in the regional office voted to do
it. But actually the information is superfluous. Any
ranger who doesn't know the places that need work
in his district without the aid of computers should be
replaced."

I think I can guess the real reasons the Forest Service requires permits. Aside from the seemingly uni-
versal compulsion to intrude on other people's lives,
to make rules that must be obeyed, the reasons are
twofold:

First, the permits are a defense mechanism. The
Forest Service is under constant pressure from the
wilderness groups not only to expand the amount of
land in the wilderness but also to keep it pure. The
permit is a demonstration that the service is dili-
gent. If the service forces citizens to have a permit,
the pressure groups can't say it is ignoring the purity
of the wilderness.

Second, the permits reassure the service that it still
has the authority to regulate the wilderness. The
pressure groups have demonstrated they have the

power to take land out of the Forest Service's hands and transfer it to the Park Service, as happened with the North Cascades.

Those same pressure groups more and more are involving themselves in the day-to-day operations of the service regarding both wilderness and nonwilderness lands, to the extent in fact that the service now submits plans before they are executed to be examined by pressure group officers.

Under those circumstances, the service really can't be completely certain just what its powers and prerogatives are. As long as it has the force to require even pressure group officers to obtain a permit before entering the wilderness, it can be reasonably assured it still is in control.[3]

The wilderness permit is only the first obstacle the hiker encounters. He also must go into the wilderness with the knowledge that he may meet a wilderness ranger at any time and that the wilderness ranger really is a cop.

Once, a couple of years ago, I accompanied one of those rangers on one of his tours of duty in the White Pass area of the Glacier Peak Wilderness. The ranger was Ben Englebright, a wiry little guy who can carry a sixty-pound pack at a fast pace uphill all day long and be ready for a couple more hours of work after dinner. Believe me, it's tough to keep up with him.

Ben, incidentally, was the first ranger assigned to the Glacier Peak Wilderness. Since that wilderness was created by the same Wilderness Act of 1964 that defined wilderness, he may have been the first wilderness ranger in the United States. He strikes one as a friendly, likeable, sincere guy who believes in what he is doing. He is, like Cal Dunnell, my kind of wilderness crusader. He once had an executive position with a major oil company. When his kids were grown, he took early retirement so he could work, at much less pay, in the wilderness. He does that during the summer. In the winter he travels and teaches part time at a local community college.

And let it not be said that Ben's only duty was to harass people in the wilderness. He also during our three days together worked hard at such jobs as clearing obstructions from the trail, digging drainage ways in the trail, reerecting fallen signs, marking trails, cleaning campsites, and picking up litter. Our packs were heavier coming out than going in and we still didn't carry out all the litter we picked up.[4]

But, despite all those other responsibilities, Ben devoted a good part of his work day to what he called public education. He would stop every person we saw, ask to see their permit, and give them a five-minute talk that sounded a great deal like the pointless spiel the clerks used to give people when they applied for a wilderness permit.

And with about the same result. On the second day we stopped a group of six or eight people. While Ben was giving his talk, one absently edged away to near where I was standing. Obviously he was less than absorbed.

"You're not listening," I observed.

"This is about the eighth time I've heard this talk," he said. He apparently had met a number of rangers in the backcountry.

Ben's assignment was and is a necessary part of wilderness management. If the land is to be frozen, left completely untrammeled, police officers must be assigned to keep it that way. That's the first step. As the popularity of outdoors and wilderness grows, the restrictions and enforcement must grow apace in severity. Eventually in any given wilderness even the most severe regimentation no longer suffices and the bureaucracy is forced to take the last step; they have to establish a maximum number of people they will

Windy Pass area of North Cascades, a favorite backcountry place of the author's family, has been declared wilderness and put under unnecessary restrictions, rules and regulations that destroy the spiritual wilderness atmosphere. Forest Service officials say they eventually will "ration" visitors (that is, limit the number of visitors) so they won't leave any sign they have been there.

allow in the wilderness and limit the permits they
issue to that number. Those who don't get a permit
try again next year. Both Park and Forest Service
officials already have begun doing just that. They
call it "rationing" the wilderness, apparently un-
aware that that is a self-contradiction.

The U.S. Park Service once decided to remove the backcountry
hostels where hikers stop for rest and a meal in Glacier Park's
backcountry. Park officials said the hostels attracted large
numbers of people who "threatened the environment." The Park
Service abandoned the plan, at least temporarily, after large
numbers of people protested that the hostels had been there for 60
years without destroying the environment.

And meantime, the regimentation and "protection" of some parks and wilderness have reached ridiculous proportions. For instance:

Officials in a Midwest wilderness have outlawed not just littering but even possession of cans and plastic containers. People who have worked there tell me that in the past they were authorized to stop people on the trail and search their packs. I understand that is not done now but if a ranger sees someone in possession of those articles the culprit is arrested.

And, officials of Glacier National Park decided to demolish the park's back country hostels where hikers can stop for a hot meal and a clean bed. They said the hostels attracted large numbers of people and those people were "threatening to destroy the fragile environment." The hostels had been there for 60 years without destroying the environment and so many people protested that the park officials changed their minds, at least temporarily.

And, officials of the Olympic National Park in Washington have allowed the buildings of the Lars Ahlstrom homestead in a forest meadow near Cape Alava to decay almost to the point of destruction. The place is the westernmost homestead in the conterminous United States and depicts the end of the nation's free land era that began in the early 1600's. Park officials say they are allowing the homestead to be destroyed by vandals and time because they think the meadow "should go back to nature."

And, the North Cascades National Park has moved to "protect the wilderness setting" of the Cascade Pass trail by erecting along its 4 mile length no less than 37 signs commanding visitors to do certain things and prohibiting them from doing certain other things.

And there was a story in the papers recently about a ranger in a national park who fired a 38-caliber

Lars Ahlstrom's homestead, in the Olympic National Park, was the westernmost homestead in the United States. It is a priceless symbol of the free land era that formed the nation's character. Yet the U. S. Park Service is letting it rot away because it believes the meadow should go back to nature.

These are a few of the thirty-seven signs the U. S. Park Service erected on the four miles of the Cascade Pass trail to "protect its wilderness setting."

REGULATIONS
NORTH CASCADES NATIONAL PARK

This partial reference to Federal Regulations is posted to assist the backcountry traveler. A complete list of regulations may be reviewed at the nearest National Park Service Office.

1. CAMPING PERMITTED ONLY AT AUTHORIZED LOCATIONS. BACKCOUNTRY USERS ARE REQUIRED TO OBTAIN A WRITTEN PERMIT BEFORE CAMPING OR LIGHTING FIRES.

2. ONLY DOWN AND DEAD WOOD MAY BE USED FOR CAMPFIRE FUEL.

3. DOGS, CATS AND OTHER PETS ARE PROHIBITED WITHIN THE NATIONAL PARK EXCEPT ON THE CASCADE CREST TRAIL.

4. THE USE OF FIREARMS IS PROHIBITED.

5. FISHING IS PERMITTED IN ACCORDANCE WITH STATE LAW.

6. PICNICKING IS PERMITTED ONLY WHERE POSTED AND IN AUTHORIZED CAMPING AREAS.

7. ALL NATURAL OBJECTS ARE PROTECTED EXCEPT THAT THE GATHERING OF BERRIES AND FRUITS FOR PERSONAL CONSUMPTION IS PERMITTED.

8. SADDLE AND PACK ANIMALS MAY NOT BE KEPT IN CAMPING AREAS.

9. MOTOR VEHICLES AND BICYCLES ARE PROHIBITED ON TRAILS.

10. HUNTING IS NOT PERMITTED.

11. OPERATING A MOTOR VEHICLE OFF THE ESTABLISHED AND MAINTAINED ROADS IS PROHIBITED.

12. EXCEPT IN EXTREME EMERGENCIES INVOLVING THE SAFETY OF HUMAN LIFE OR THREAT OF SERIOUS PROPERTY LOSS, THE AIR DELIVERY OF ANY PERSON OR THING BY PARACHUTE, HELICOPTER OR OTHER MEANS WITHOUT PRIOR WRITTEN PERMISSION OF THE SUPERINTENDENT IS PROHIBITED.

13. BURN ALL REFUSE AND PACK OUT YOUR NONCOMBUSTIBLES. DO NOT BURY YOUR TRASH.

PETS PROHIBITED ON ALL TRAILS

bullet into a mechanical snow vehicle because he feared the driver might go into an area where such machines are prohibited.

And in the past several years the Forest Service and Park Service have destroyed at least four Adirondack shelters and cabins in the North Cascades. The structures were erected years ago by rangers and Civilian Conservation Corps men to provide shelter for hikers and rangers. The buildings were destroyed in response to the pressure groups' demand that the Wilderness Act prohibition of any sign of man be strictly adhered to.

And in California recently the Forest Service removed the pit toilets from a popular trail to the peak of Mount Whitney because the toilets failed to blend with the environment. Then they closed the trail to all but seventy-five persons a day because they found the campgrounds littered with excrement. Thousands of people were barred from the trail. "It's a tough thing when you have to restrict the public from public land," a Forest Service spokesman said.

And the Forest Service recently allowed the Sierra Club to recruit a group of young people from California to clean up litter in Washington's North Cascades. Later it turned out that what the youngsters "cleaned up" were historical artifacts from some of the old mining areas. The youngsters proudly boasted that they destroyed at the sites as much as possible of the priceless reminders of the nation's heritage. The rest they carried out of the mountains to the garbage dump. The Forest Service belatedly announced it would enforce the laws designed to protect such historical treasures on public lands.

And take the case of what happened to some friends and me when we hiked several years ago over Park Creek Pass across the Cascades shortly after

The door of a wood stove is picked from the snow-crushed ruins of a shack in a mine area abandoned early in the century. A Sierra Club sponsored group boasted that they had destroyed similar historical artifacts while "cleaning up" a Cascade Mountain area.

the North Cascades National Park was created from Forest Service land. It was one of those bad luck hikes, three days and two nights and it rained just about every step of the way. Everything went well— if uncomfortably—until we got to the crest of Park Creek Pass. The fog was so thick we could see only ten to twenty feet. The pass was a popular camping ground and is the hub not just for the main trail but for lateral trails to climbs and back country areas. There was a maze of trails at the top and we couldn't tell in the fog which led to the Fisher Creek trail where we were headed.

After a few moments of wandering we couldn't find

our way back to the Park Creek trail on which we had
hiked to the pass. That left us completely dis-
oriented. We spent more than an hour walking into
dead ends and false leads. The fog got thicker, the
wind became cold, and the rain turned to sleet. It
began to look like we were going to spend an uncom-
fortable night waiting for the fog to lift. Then,
through pure luck, we stumbled on a hole in the
ground next to a junction in the trail. It was trian-
gular with walls perpendicular to the ground and
appeared to be an empty post hole. We looked around
and, sure enough, found a sign hidden in some
bushes. It bore several notations including one with
an arrow giving the direction to the Fisher Creek
trail. Fortunately the post was a right-angled triangle
so we were able to fit it into the post hole in its
original position and that told us which way to go.

We finished the hike wondering what kind of
vandals would hide a trail sign. And why.

Months later, at a meeting in Everett, a friend of
mine from the Park Service showed a program of
slides on the new North Cascades Park. He told how
the wilderness-conservation groups had complained
that the Forest Service had littered the mountains
with signs that showed the intrusion of man in the
mountains. So, he explained, the Park Service when
it took over from the Forest Service had removed
many of the signs left by the Forest Service. Then he
flashed a slide on the screen showing a park ranger
dragging the Park Creek Pass sign down the trail to
be hidden in the bushes "until we could come back
and carry it out."

It turned out my friend who was giving the program had also taken the picture. After the program I
told him what had happened to my party. He thought
it over and decided removing signs may have been
overenthusiastic. I've hiked with him and worked

with him extensively since and I like to tease him
about the sign. He just smiles and says next time he'll
change the sign to lead me over a thousand-foot cliff.

Possibly the most wasteful result of the wilderness
preservation practices is the new policy of allowing
forest fires to burn unchecked. Both the Park Service
and the Forest Service, of course, ban all logging on
lands they manage as wilderness. They justify that
on the basis that they have a responsibility to maintain the forests in their "virgin" condition. They have
heard and have heeded the wilderness-conservationists cry that a logged forest and especially a
clearcut forest is a "destroyed" forest and has become
"lost" forever. They also, in the past, have automatically rushed to put out any fires that occur in the
wilderness forests.

Forests, of course, are made up of living trees. It is
their nature to eventually die. Nature's way of weed-
ing out a forest is by fire. Man's way is by logging.
The park and forest rangers discovered that when
they banned both logging and fire, they were causing
unexpected problems. Most wild animals, for example, don't fare well in mature forests. They need the
openness and browse of the clearings.[5] Then, too, the
heat of the fire releases nutrients in the soil and
provides other resources valuable to the natural
cycle.

Recognizing this, the Park and Forest Service
recently have established a new policy of allowing
forest fires, in wilderness areas and under certain
conditions, to go unchecked. That puts society in the
position of denying itself the product of the forest to
maintain the forest's "virginity" but letting that same
forest be destroyed by fire. Some argue, of course,
that clearcutting does not provide the heat necessary for some of the benefits of a forest fire. Usually,
however, in the Northwest forests, at least, clearcut
areas are cleared of the "slash" material (the residue

of unmarketable branches and rotted wood) left by the loggers through burning. The heat of the slash fire provides the same benefits as the heat of a forest fire. And the harvest that precedes a slash fire has the added benefits of providing the wood needed for products humanity uses plus the jobs required to harvest and process the trees into useable goods.

Allowing that raw material and those jobs to go up, literally, in smoke is sheer waste. The smoke, too, is detrimental. Slash fires are burned in such a way and under such conditions that, unless something goes wrong, the smoke goes harmlessly into the upper atmosphere. Forest fires burn any way and any time and often cause air pollution far worse than most people can imagine. Even a relatively small forest fire may fill entire valleys for scores of miles in all directions with smoke so thick that motorists must drive with their headlights on at noon.

Sometimes, even when it is being fought, a forest fire may continue to destroy wood and pollute the air for weeks at a time. Unfought, it may go for months before a heavy rain puts it out or it simply destroys all of the available trees and there is nothing left to burn. The Arctic Creek fire of 1970 in the North Cascades National Park, for instance, burned from July to October while the park rangers ignored it except for an occasional flight overhead "to see how it is going."

Then, take the case of Bob Caldwell. Bob is a lawyer by education but now is in the securities business. He raises horses on his farm north of Everett, and rides them deep into the mountains every chance he gets. He is from Montana and he used to take the horses back there each summer to reexplore some of his old haunts in the Rockies. A couple of years ago he went on such a trip in a Montana wilderness. When he came back, he was an angry man.

First, he said, he had met another party of horse-

Fire is nature's way of clear cutting a forest to make way for a new generation. But allowing a forest to be removed by fire instead of harvesting wastes the wood and results in smoke pollution of the atmosphere for many miles.

men on the wilderness trail and they warned him to "be careful of the rangers." They had been stopped, the horesemen told him, for an infraction of the wilderness rules, they weren't sure just what. The ranger had written an arrest citation, then collected $50 "fine" on the spot.[6] It was fortunate that the horsemen happened to have $50 cash with them. Otherwise, apparently, they would have been forced to ride out of the wilderness to wait in jail until either they raised the money or the court made other arrangements.

Bob and his companions commiserated with the other party and rode on. A couple days later they met a ranger on the trail. He stopped to chat in a friendly sort of way.

During the course of the conversation the ranger said he wanted to congratulate Bob and his companions on their campfire of the previous night. He told them it was exactly the right kind of fire and listed the things they had done right.

Bob thanked the ranger. "But," he asked, "how did you know? You weren't anywhere near us."

The ranger explained that he had been on the ridge above their camp, watching, apparently with high-powered glasses. The concept of police spying in the wilderness shocked Bob. It concerned his wife, Gloria, too. Restrooms in the wilderness consist of a bush somewhere near camp. "I wanted to ask him what else he saw," Gloria said when they got back, "but I was afraid of what he would say."

I think Bob and Gloria originally favored the wilderness program. They don't any more. They have stopped going to their old haunts in Montana and stick to the nonwilderness areas near home. But more and more of those areas are being grabbed up as wilderness, and Bob and Gloria have become active in a horsemen's group that is a leader in fighting the addition of more land into wilderness.

I doubt that either Bob or Gloria would approve of the elimination of all wilderness but their experience has shown them that the formal dedication of more wilderness-by-fiat is the greatest threat to their being able to enjoy the public land that should be available to all.

Searching hikers, destroying buildings, hiding signs, allowing valuable forests to burn, closing trails, shooting machines, "fining" people without trial and spying on citizens are not the kinds of things that happen every day. They are excessive examples of what can happen. But they are illustrative—if exaggerations—of the kind of restrictions and enforcement the bureaucracy must impose if it is to preserve the wilderness in its "untrammeled" state.

The problem is that most Americans don't visit the wilderness, don't experience overregulation and indignities that ever more frequently are becoming part of a visit to the wilderness. Few people of Chicago or New York, for instance, will ever see a dedicated wilderness. Most of those who do will content themselves with driving around it, looking at it from afar. They are likely to learn little about it. Why should they unless they have a definite interest? It is not part of their regular environment. They have other, different concerns in their everyday lives.

Their opinions will likely be based almost entirely on the incessant barrage of wilderness-conservation propaganda to which they are exposed. Wilderness has become a cause célèbre in the land. Even the most prestigious publications and networks have taken up the campaign with articles and programs to sell the pressure groups' politics. They do it because they are expected to.

Wilderness has become a popular point of interest. Editors and producers know that to be read and watched they must follow the popular trends—tell people what they want to be told, what they expect to be told. It is a snowball. The pressure groups' propaganda established a thought pattern that became widespread in the nation. Because that concept is widespread, other parts of the media—not really part of the propaganda movement—repeat the propaganda because it has become a "good story" and it is an easy way to gain an audience. And, of course, the government responds by locking up more and more land because that's what the people think they want.

And those of us who love the mountains, Bob and Gloria, and my family and I can only stand helpless and watch while the mountains are closed off to us. Helpless and voiceless. When we try to be heard, the public shuts us out because everyone knows that wilderness is good and more wilderness is better. And the pressure groups attack us as agents of the "commercial interests."

CHAPTER SEVEN

Originally about 11 million acres of land were declared wilderness under the Wilderness Act of 1964, not counting millions more which are managed as wilderness even though Congress has not declared them to be wilderness. The pressure groups act as if that 11 million acres are insignificant but actually it is more than the combined area of Rhode Island, New Jersey, and Connecticut.

After the act was passed another 11 million acres were designated to be actively considered for wilderness. About 5 million of those acres have been added to the declared wilderness areas. There appears little chance Congress will not eventually include the rest. That adds an area the size of Massachusetts and New Hampshire to the other three states.

How much more will be added? It depends on

whose guess you accept. Frome, in his Wilderness Society sponsored book, *Battle for the Wilderness*,[1] talks about 50 to 60 million acres in various categories—national parks and monuments, national wildlife refuges, and national forests. That would add the equivalent of New York state to the five states mentioned above. Then Frome goes on to talk about "a much broader potential"[2] for wilderness being discovered by later studies. Just how much broader, he doesn't say. But during a press conference in June 1976, U. S. Forest Service Chief John McGuire guessed there might be as much as 80 million acres in wilderness eventually. That would add Maine and Maryland.

J. Michael McCloskey, executive director of the Sierra Club, in a speech to the Northwest Wilderness Conference in 1974 called for as much as 200 million acres. Add Illinois, Indiana, and Michigan.

I've heard it said by an industry source—and therefore admittedly a biased source—that some wilderness conservationists have 400 million acres of wilderness as their goal. If so, add Iowa, Nevada, South Carolina, Wisconsin, and Washington. That brings us to a total of 16 states—one-sixth of all the land area in the United States—set aside for the exclusive recreation of a small group of well-to-do, middle-class elite and their drop-out supporters.

But it doesn't really stop there. The wilderness-conservation pressure groups' appetite is insatiable. They won't stop until someone stops them. They can't. To stop campaigning for wilderness would be to discard the major reason the organizations exist. The profit seekers need the organizations because they provide their jobs and incomes. Pressure relievers need the organizations because they provide a means for building their power base and their egos. The profit seekers and pressure relievers largely control the pressure groups. There is little chance they will allow the groups to slacken the pace regardless of how much land Congress declares wilderness.

Pittsburg Landing in Hell's Canyon became wilderness in 1976. Wilderness pressure groups must continue to demand ever more wilderness areas; to stop would be to discard the major reason the groups exist.

There is, of course, an alternative to unlimited wilderness. One the pressure groups won't like because it serves the people and the nation rather than the groups' interests. It is, nevertheless, the kind of alternative that the Congress and administration must sooner or later adopt. They represent all the people rather than only the tiny minority of wilderness-conservationists who make up the pressure groups. Sooner or later, the general public will discover that its interests have been betrayed. Then there will be a reaction. The danger is that the reaction may be too strong, that it will cause the pendulum to swing too far in the other direction. People will find themselves regimented in the wilderness where they go to be free of regimentation. Or they will find themselves barred from entering the wilderness at all because they did not apply soon enough for a permit. They may well be so repelled that they reject the wilderness system entirely. If eventually their numbers are great enough the total wilderness system could be jeopardized.

(I am not alone in my fear of a backlash to the environmental movement. In August 1973 Russell Train, during the Senate hearings on his appointment as administrator of the Environmental Protection Agency, said he was concerned over the possibility the nation's environmental programs might be swept away by public resentment.)

The longer we wait, the more land we declare wilderness, the more we regulate people on that land, the more the pressure builds. More pressure means more chance that the explosion, when it occurs, will be destructive.

The alternative is simple, really:

Put a limit on the land frozen under the present Wilderness Act. Use the rest of the public land for varying kinds of intermixed commercial and recreational purposes. The intermixture should be based on the need for recreation and the need for industrial raw materials and on the ability of the land to serve those purposes. The decisions must be based on the needs of all the people, including the vast majority who do not belong to pressure groups, do not attend public hearings, do not write letters to government officials, and do not sign petitions.[3]

The key to the intermixture of uses is the ability of the land to support the various uses and how well those uses serve society. Some of the high country meadowland that might be trampled or otherwise changed by visitors should be closed off by wilderness classification but not all of it, not so much that most people are barred from visiting that kind of country when they want to. Most of even that land should be left open for spiritual wilderness use, even though its character may be altered to some degree.

Some, also, of the hardier, lowland forest and high, rocky peaks should be set aside as land wilderness, just so we can say we have some, even though to do so we have to bar ourselves from the right to visit it much. Permits, rationing, regulations, and wilderness rangers in large measures and great strictness will be necessary to maintain that land as wilderness.

But most—nearly all—of the public land should be divided into various other levels of recreation use, compatible with the nation's need for raw materials. At one end of the recreation spectrum should be land devoted entirely to use as spiritual wilderness, left open, if it lends itself to that purpose, for commercial uses, but also for recreation, for hiking, backpacking, or whatever it is useable for. If it is not appropriate for commercial use, if the forests are not suitable for harvest, if the rocks contain no valuable minerals, if the vegetation is such that it won't support livestock, and if it is not designated for land wilderness, then it should be devoted entirely to spiritual wilderness, open without limit for hikers and backpackers. Some of it, at least, should also be given over to people who are barred or inhibited from visiting the present wilderness; horsemen, trail bikers, four-wheel-drive enthusiasts, people who like to fly into the backcountry. It should be left open for use by any citizen who wants it, with a minimum of rules, regulations, laws, and police enforcement.

And the people responsible for the land should manage it for that kind of use. If a popular spot is "loved to death" and beginning to show wear, the managers should, instead of keeping people out as they do now, make accommodations to them. If a trail shows wear, it should be rebuilt to accept the number of people who use it. If a popular camping spot becomes worn, the managers, instead of ordering people away, should put in "hardened" campsites of gravel, wood chips, or whatever. If an area develops a sanitation problem, the managers should put in privies to solve the problem instead of "restricting the public from the public land" as the National Forest officials did to the Mt. Whitney trail.

The land that is commercially useable should be opened to that use but it should be kept open also to recreational uses. Land that can be used for grazing livestock should be so used. We need the meat, wool, leather, and other products. But precautions should be taken that the stock owners do not allow the land to be overgrazed so it becomes unable to recover and graze another generation of stock. And while the stock is off the land, or even while it is on the land if that is feasible, the area should remain open to recreational use.

Mining also should be permitted where it is in the people's economic interest. But it should be regulated so that it disrupts the land as little as possible, so that it has little effect on recreation.

Indeed, such restrictions on mining are in effect now. Pressure groups like to point to Holden Mine above Lake Chelan in Eastern Washington as an example of what happens when mining is permitted. The Holden Mine was poorly operated from an environmental standpoint. The loose tailings were dumped in a huge mound and held to the sloping landscape by wooden pilings. The pilings are rotting out and the tailings are eroding into the stream causing pollution that effects fish in part of the stream below the mine.

A herd of sheep moves to a grazing area in the Hell's Canyon wilderness. Wilderness groups are bringing pressure to outlaw sheep here even though sheepherding is a long established tradition in the area and provides the country with wool and food.

The wilderness-environmentalist propagandists love to describe Holden Mine as typical of mining in the mountains. They neglect to say that the mine was opened in 1937 and closed in 1957. Since then, the government has laid down strict rules and regulations that would make it impossible to operate a mine the way Holden Mine was operated. As a matter of fact, miners today are forced to go to extreme lengths to protect the environment. The chances of their causing extensive permanent damage are negligible.

The reality is that mines are interesting places and those that operate on public land should make themselves available for such recreation oriented activities as tours of the mines. When they are exhausted and close down, their buildings should be turned over to the public for use as museums, hotels, or backcountry hostels. Indeed, the Holden Mine left its facilities intact and they have been used for years by a church group as a backcountry resort.

A mother and her son pause in a tunnel of a long abandoned railroad to a Cascade Mountain mining area. Railroads, roads and other mine appurtenances can be used as hiking facilities when the mines close.

Facilities at other mines could be designed for eventual use by the government. The mine roads and railroads for example, can be closed, allowed to revert to nature and become foot trails. The mine structures could then be used as chalets or hostels to provide rest and food for hikers.

And forests, too, can be used both for recreation and for supplying people with houses, paper, plastics, and other needed goods.

Many Americans find it difficult to grasp the concept of renewable forests. From the beginning of our national experience, forests have been looked on as nonrenewable. Once they were harvested, we walked away from them to find another forest to cut. Some of the former forest land was farmed but most of it was held to be exhausted wasteland. Only a generation ago land where I live was being sold by logging companies for a few dollars an acre. Often there were no takers and the land was allowed to go to the county for unpaid taxes.

That wasteland attitude is ingrained into our national attitude, along with the false premise that there always is another forest to be cut. Once, it was only necessary to move West to unused land areas and find a new forest. Now that we have run out of West, we see the concept is not valid.

Forests, once harvested, regrow. The land can be used over and over again to grow new forests. Indeed, even if we don't harvest them, eventually they will die and burn and regrow naturally.

And the regrowing forest provides a magnificent opportunity for recreation. Once logged, for instance, a valley can be closed off, the roads blocked, and the valley used as a hikers' avenue to the high country.

The pressure group propagandists like to publish photographs of clearcut forests to persuade the country that clearcuts are ugly. Actually the photographs often are composed and processed in a way especially designed to make the scene ugly. The truth is that even if clearcuts are not attractive the year

During the 1940s a logger, using only his axe and saw, carved the figure of a "Maid of the Woods" on a tall cedar snag in the midst of a clearcut harvest area. Now new trees have grown so tall the old snag is nearly hidden from view. Forests, once harvested, regrow. And if they are not harvested, they burn, then regrow.

after the loggers are finished, they become beautiful during the years after that.

Nature's process is to rebuild a forest in stages. The first stage is a carpet of wildflowers, led in my part of the world by the tall, stately, purple fireweed, so named because it is one of the first plants to appear after a forest has burned. The carpet of brightly colored flowers may contrast with the gaunt grey stumps and limbs left by the loggers.[4] In the background are the distant slopes and peaks of the mountains. The sky is bright blue or dull grey, depending on the weather. Often at dawn and dusk the sunrise or sunset paints the sky in magnificent colors that rival even the carpet of flowers.

The beauty of such a scene is unimaginable. Some of the most pleasant camping trips my family and I have spent have been in an old clearcut.

In a few years brush and bushes replace the flowers. This land cover varies with the seasons from deep green to brilliant red. The bushes that produce the luscious huckleberry frequently abound. Often in the fall my family and I have spent entire days picking a supply of berries for winter's pies and cereals and sundaes. Sometimes there are other people about, but usually we are alone. Sometimes we set up camp and stay overnight. And the wilderness-conservationists' claim that clearcuts are ugly is not borne out by our immensely satisfying experience.

Then, of course, after the brush, the trees return. Often, in my part of the country, the alder comes first. A deciduous legume, it tends to put nitrogen in the soil. Then it dies out and is replaced by the conifers that give Washington its nickname of Evergreen State.

If the clearcut forest is replanted by man, in the Northwest, it probably will be replanted with evergreens. That eliminates the alder or other deciduous trees. It doesn't matter. Within a few years a new young forest replaces the old and the beauty is the same as it was before the loggers arrived. When the new forest matures, it can be cut again.

The author's wife, Eleanor, picks a winter's supply of huckleberries in a clearcut forest. Berry bushes grow amidst young Douglas fir trees planted a few years earlier by foresters. The colors of the berry bush leaves and wildflowers combine with the mountain view to make clearcuts places of beauty, contrary to wilderness pressure groups' propaganda.

Meantime the forest can be used through all its stages for recreation of many kinds, including a primitive kind of spiritual wilderness.

In a way, the wilderness-conservationists have admitted the feasibility of using and reusing the forests for both commercial and recreation purposes. Once, in the early days of their campaign, they repeated often the battle cry that "once lost, it is lost forever." That implied that if the forest was harvested, it could never again be suitable for wilderness or recreation.

That remained part of the propaganda for a long time. But eventually the program became so successful that the pressure groups could see they soon would have all the "virgin" land available. That left them with the alternative of going out of business or expanding their target to include land already contributing to the nation's economic well being.

Going out of business, of course, was unthinkable. It meant hunting for other employment and other ways to feed the ego. So for the past few years we have heard less of the "once gone, gone forever" slogan and we hear more and more about the ability of the land to heal itself. It we lock it up, they now tell us, it will restore itself to its original condition and can be declared wilderness. They never add that soon thereafter the rangers will begin erecting their "keep out" signs.

There are more gradations to recreational use of the land than just land and spiritual wildernesses. A full spectrum would include camping of the tent and trailer varieties, hunting, fishing, boating, canoeing, nature walks, historical hikes and displays, and so forth. But these enjoyments are possible only if the people can prevent so much of their land being locked up that there is not enough left for them to enjoy.

The concept of rebuilding the forest and using the land for multiple levels of recreation is not new. Nor is it original with me. A couple of years ago, for instance, when Cal Dunnell was recreation staff assistant of the Mount Baker National Forest, I visited him in his office and we resumed our favorite topic of discussion: arguing over the recreational use of the forest.

I told him of my ideas for multiple recreation. He got up from his desk, reached behind a bookcase, and pulled out a large pasteboard poster. On it were listed numerous levels of recreation the land in the Mount Baker Forest would be suitable for.

He told me the Forest Service, some years earlier, made a trial-balloon proposal to establish specific areas of the Mount Baker forest for each of the levels. Cal and other forest officials made the proposal during a public meeting, using the poster to illustrate the plan. The pressure groups reacted, negatively, with such vigor that next day Cal put the poster behind the bookcase. I doubt that it had ever come out again until my visit. Wilderness-conservationists want no land-use programs that make the public land available to anyone but themselves. For any purposes but their own. Then or now.

The National Park Service has a similar plan for gradations of recreation uses of the land. Theirs calls for six levels of use and is similar to the Forest Service's in its object of serving the people who own the land. That plan, too, was attacked by the pressure groups.[5] For all practical purposes, it has been hidden away ever since.

The multi-purpose, multi-recreational use of the public land, incidentally, is in complete harmony with the land managers' responsibility to maintain the wildlife and water resources. Many animals thrive better in cleared areas than in dense forests. Clearcuts, obviously, enhance their environment. Indeed, many animals seem to thrive near the trails where they are most apt to see people.

Those wild animals that prefer forest cover would have it available in the regrown forests. The forests should be harvested and regrown in tracts large enough so that animals that eschew the presence of man have opportunity to remain as aloof as they like.

Trees, of course, should be harvested so as to eliminate danger of polluting the streams and lakes in the forest and to prevent destruction of the fish habitat in those waters. Despite pressure groups' horror propaganda about muddy waters and dead fish, there are techniques for logging without harming streams. Those techniques are required by law now, and the laws are strictly enforced.

One problem regarding the multi-recreation use of the public land is that it will open the land to more people to enjoy. That implies the expense of more trails, campgrounds, toilets, and so on. The Forest Service and Park Service both are hard pressed to find the funds to provide and maintain facilities for use at the present level. Congress has shown no great enthusiasm for appropriating more funds and adding to already unmanageable budget deficits.

But maybe that's just as well. There is no reason why the people who use the public lands shouldn't do much of the work themselves. It can be done on an organized-group basis, and, indeed many organizations even now are helping. Some, such as the Student Conservation Association, devote themselves almost entirely to working on trails, bridges, campgrounds, and so forth. As a matter of fact, if the wilderness-conservation pressure groups would devote to improving the public lands the energy they give to stealing it, there might not be a land-for-recreation shortage at all.

Bighorn sheep, mountain
goats, elk, and marmots all
posed for author's camera.
Many wild animals seem to
thrive near trails where
they are most apt to see
people.

Individuals and families can work in the public lands, too. My family and I, for instance, have helped to do the maintenance work on a trail in the North Cascades. We devoted several weeks to it. We weren't anywhere near as efficient as a professional crew. But there was no crew available and, if we hadn't done it, it might not have been done.

Many parks and national forests have people assigned to working with volunteers, giving them assignments, instructions, helping them in whatever way they need. It's a great way to spend part of a vacation and if enough people do it, there won't be any budget problem for the land managers to fret about.

A multiple-level recreation program, obviously, requires that the amount of area locked up in land wilderness be limited. The decision on how much should properly be given that classification must of necessity be arbitrary. A million acres would not be enough. The 16 million acres now in wilderness may not be enough. The additional 6 million acres now formally proposed for wilderness are probably too much, although there seems little chance they can be saved. Michael Frome's proposal that at least 50 million acres be locked up is grossly unreasonable. Michael McCloskey's proposal to the wilderness convention that 200 million acres go to land wilderness is preposterous, so immensely irrational that it becomes an insult to the nation and the intelligence of its people.

Whatever the amount, the decision will have to be made by Congress. It should make that decision quickly and at the same time set the general outlines for multi-use, multi-level recreation of the rest of the public lands. Then it should let the public agencies manage the land under those policies so that the people may use and enjoy it.

CHAPTER EIGHT

———————◆———————

This is a book about ideas, about the concepts of political equity and democracy, about the use or misuse of power and public trust. Let me sum up by telling three stories.

First story, Hap Annen and his mountain:

I'm not sure what Hap's real first name was. I don't think I ever heard it. He was called Hap or Happy because he smiled and laughed frequently. He was a big man, his motions were quick, his stride fast and long, his voice deep and loud. He loved life and people and the world and he enjoyed being what he was. His name was a natural.

Hap's home, when I knew him, was on a high bank on the east side of Everett. The view looked out over the Snohomish Valley directly at the huge bulk of Mount Pilchuck. I think Hap told me he grew up in that house. At any rate, he grew up somewhere there-abouts and when he was young he would look at Mount Pilchuck and wonder. He would wonder what it was like on top. Whether anyone had ever been there. How a person could get to the top. Somehow the little boy built a fascination for the huge moun-tain that stayed with him all his life.

Actually Mount Pilchuck is not especially high. But it lies at the end of a spur that juts westward from the Cascades. It is so close to Everett that it seems to dominate the mountain range. The peak is snow covered most of the year, and on a clear day it is so obvious a part of the view that it seems almost a part of the city.

When Hap became old enough he began to visit the mountain. He visited the low forests first, then higher places. Finally he climbed it, an adventure he was to repeat many scores of times in his lifetime.

When Hap grew up, he became an auto mechanic and eventually owned his own repair shop. He never lost his fascination for the mountain. He visited other parts of the Cascades. Indeed, he was active in obtaining some pieces of land that were donated to the Forest Service as campgrounds. But he always returned to Pilchuck as his favorite grounds. He explored every nook, every shoulder, every ridge. After a fire lookout was built on the peak, he took several summers off to work in it.

Hap's love for the mountain was not selfish. He did not try to keep it to himself, devise ways to keep other people away. Instead, he worked hard to open the mountain to people. It is a beautiful, magnificent mountain, and Hap wanted everyone to know it.

When the state opened a ski area on Pilchuck's slopes, Hap was overjoyed, although he was critical of the location. If they had built it only a few hun-dred yards away, he told me, they would have had better slopes, better snow, and more space for parking.

He worked hard to get new trails built on the mountain and in some cases, used saw and axe himself to help.

But Hap did not live to see his biggest dream for the mountain realized. When he was young there were mountain goats on the high parts of the mountain. Sometime before World War II they disappeared. Hunted out, some said. They overpopulated and destroyed their own habitat, according to others. No matter. If the habitat had been destroyed it had restored itself. Hap had researched mountain goats and was convinced that they could thrive there. He developed a plan for transplanting goats from some other area where the animals were crowding their habitat.

Hap was already old when I knew him, long retired from his business but still carrying on his love affair with his mountain. Often he would talk about his plans and hopes for improving it and getting more people up to enjoy it.

One day he took me to the ski area and told me about his goat transplant dream. He said the State Game Department had agreed to make the transplant but nothing had happened.

I wrote a story for the *Herald*'s Saturday magazine about Hap's plan to transplant goats. The magazine then had a lead time of three or four weeks. The story was delayed for several reasons, including my own procrastination in writing it. The time lapsed into months and the story still had not run. I knew it would eventually and I wasn't concerned. Hap was used to the daily news operation, and he didn't understand the delay even though I explained it to him.

One day Hap came into the office, obviously not

himself. The smile was less deep. He laughed less boisterously. The stride was slower, shorter. He didn't seem like the real Hap. I asked if anything was wrong. He shrugged and said he had been to the doctor that morning and doctors always left him feeling a little blue. He asked again about the goat story. I told him not to worry. It would come out when the editor was good and ready. Hap was obviously disappointed. He went away sadly.

I never saw him again. Next I heard about him, he had died. The story ran about the same time and I'm not certain whether Hap saw it.

I felt bad about Hap after he died. I wrote the story about the goats because I thought it was a "good story," not to put pressure on the Game Department. Nevertheless, his idea was a good one, and I wish the story had run sooner for his sake.

A year or so later I climbed Pilchuck with my wife and a couple of our daughters. The trail begins at the ski area and winds up through some thick stands of old-growth timber. It is an obvious trail there. But when it reaches the subalpine fir elevations it gets into an area of glaciated rock slabs where no amount of travel will ever wear a trail.

Many years earlier, Hap had taken a can of yellow paint up the mountain and marked the trail over the rocks. He painted on the rocks arrows and messages of direction, even messages of encouragement such as "keep going" and "it isn't far now." Hap always felt that as many people as possible should enjoy his mountain as much as possible. He hated the thought that someone might turn back before they got to the peak.

On that day my family and I climbed the mountain, I got out ahead of the others and stopped to wait on a pleasant little shoulder just above treeline. We had been up Pilchuck many times and I knew Hap's

yellow trail markers were ahead. Still, it's a good
idea to stick together in a place like that. So I waited.

While I was waiting another hiker came down the
trail. When he approached the rock where I was sitting, I spoke and asked him how it was going. He
stopped and in a tone of exasperation said, "some
vandal has slopped yellow paint on the rocks up
there." Then he launched into a dissertation on
"mindless vandalism" and the people who "have no
respect for nature." He repeated the tired old propaganda slogans of the wilderness pressure groups,
telling me that the mountains should be untouched
and should bear no sign of man's presence. The paint
spots, he claimed, endangered the environment and
the ecology and damaged the untouched pristine
setting and spoiled the majestic beauty of the mountain which he said is unique and delicate. He said his
wilderness experience had been destroyed by seeing
those painted trail markers and that anyone who
would scar the mountain with paint was stupid.

I listened for awhile. Then I'm afraid I lost my cool.
Usually I'm pretty even tempered but maybe I was
feeling a little guilt for not trying to get the goat story
published before Hap died. I told the man off.

I told him about Hap and why Hap marked the trail
and how much Hap had loved the mountain. And
before I was half through, I realized that I was
making a mistake.

I'll never forget his expression. He was surprised at
my outburst, shocked. He was dismayed and puzzled.
And suddenly I realized he hadn't really meant what
he had said.

It came on me all at once that in all probability
what the man was doing was starting a conversation. He had said what he said about Hap's marks
because he had assumed that such criticism was
universally accepted, that everyone, and especially

someone who was halfway up the mountain, would agree that Hap's marks were vandalism. It suddenly came to me that everything he said had come directly from the pressure groups' propaganda mill. He simply was repeating the concepts, even the language of the pressure groups' publications and speeches. He was so completely brainwashed by the propaganda that he was sure everyone in the country would agree.

It never occurred to him that anyone would not accept what he was saying. He had said it simply to establish a common ground so that I could respond in kind and we could exchange ideas on a noncontroversial subject while we rested a moment on the trail. His attack on Hap had simply been another way of saying, "It's a nice day, isn't it," and giving me a chance to respond.

His remarks had been a friendly overture and I responded in an entirely unfriendly way. He was disturbed and shocked and he backed off, mumbled something like an apology and took off down the trail. He had been quite right in assuming that most Americans would consider Hap's marks to be vandalism. That is one of the crimes of the pressure groups' propagandists. They have people believing there is something wrong with loving a mountain, that it is evil to want to share a mountain with others.

Second story, Red Bridge:

Recently, my wife, my daughter Meri and I spent a weekend camping at Red Bridge Campground in the Mount Baker-Snoqualmie National Forest. The campground is on the bank of the South Fork of the Stillaguamish River. One afternoon, while the sun was low, I wandered up the river to try to get a picture with shadows and highlights on the water in the background. I found a place that looked like it might be productive in a moment when the sun shifted. I sat on the bank to wait.

There was a family of people on the low, sandy bank on the other side of the river. The father was knee deep in the river, fishing perhaps fifty yards upstream. The mother was sitting on a rock on the bank behind him. Three children were playing in the sand directly across from me. A little girl, about four, was standing at the water's edge waving a branch and dipping it into the water in approximate imitation of her father's actions with the fishing rod. Nearby a boy about seven and a girl slightly older were digging in the sand and rock of the beach.

The smaller girl waved her stick back and forth until it hit the water, splashing a few drops on the older children. The older children giggled and the little girl looked around and saw what she had done. She laughed and smacked the stick into the water again. Water splashed up, but nowhere near the children. The boy shouted and dashed to the water's edge, daring her to splash water on him. She made another swipe at the river. The boy dodged away, then jumped back to give her another chance. They did that several times, then the older girl joined the boy. The two would stand at the water's edge dancing until the little girl smacked the water with her stick; then they would run screaming up the bank to escape the splash.

Upstream, the mother, hearing the shouts, stood to watch her brood. After a few moments the youngsters tired of the game. The little girl walked to the hole the other children had been digging and shoved her stick into it. Then all three worked to fill the hole and pile rocks around the stick which jutted upright. What had moments before been a fishing rod became a flag pole or perhaps a tree. The mother sat down and resumed watching her husband fish.

It became apparent the sun was not going to oblige

with the scene I had in mind so I wandered away. Sadly. I couldn't help but think that family is what the wilderness-conservationists consider the enemy.

It is just such people as that family that the wilderness-conservationists have in mind when they talk about "loving a place to death." It is just such people that the pressure groups have in mind when they seek to lock up the land. It is just such people that will be harmed by the pressure groups' drive for power and hunger for the people's land.

Red Bridge campground would be closed if the area became part of a wilderness.

Red Bridge is not in a wilderness, of course. It is a developed campground beside a relatively well-developed road. But the campground and the road are deep within the Cascades and the pressure groups already have begun aiming their propaganda at declaring developed areas to be wilderness and letting them go back to nature. There is some privately owned land near Red Bridge but Congress and the pressure groups have long since established the practice of forcing private land owners to sell or have their land condemned for wilderness. Land on both sides of Red Bridge is under study for wilderness. It would be only a small step to take Red Bridge, too.

That, of course, would mean the campground would be closed and so would the road. People could get there only if they chose to go on foot, and put up with the Forest Service's massive list of rules and regulations. The camper the little family had in the campground would be outlawed and, unless they changed to conform to the pressure groups' definition of a rewarding outdoor experience, so would they.

Third story, White Chuck Valley:

Last summer Meri and I took a day hike up an old abandoned logging road in the White Chuck Valley.

The road begins in a campground and the first couple hundred yards are well used. But the logging has been finished for several years and the road has not been maintained so drivers of most vehicles find it too rough to go very far.

After the first couple hundred yards there were no tracks except for those of a motorcycle and a vehicle which I assume was a four-wheel drive of some kind. The road became rougher, the further we walked. Flowers, grass, brush, small trees had grown in the roadway. Occasionally, there were dried ponds in a

low spot of the tread. In a few places water running
in the tread had eroded shallow ditches. But when it
washed away the dirt, the water left the heavier
rocks and stones until they formed a protective layer
of gravel on the bottom of the ditch. Small plants
were beginning to find footholds among the stones.
The erosion scars were beginning the healing process. Nature has her ways. She has been eroding the
White Chuck Valley since the Cascades were formed
millions of years before man evolved. But she sets her
own pace. Man can interfere but she is patient and
wise. If he makes mistakes, she'll find a way to repair
the damage. Someday she'll flatten the Cascades to
sea level as she has twice before. But not yet. Not
until she's ready.

The four-wheeled vehicle got a half mile or so up
the road. A winter storm had dropped a tree across
the pathway. The tracks told the story. The driver
had put his bumper against the tree and tried to push
it out of the way. He moved it a few feet, then it
lodged against another tree. He spun his wheels and
threw dirt down the road. Then he gave up, backed
around, and headed toward the campground.

The motorcycle driver was able to get his bike
around the fallen tree and drive on. He made it for
another mile, encountering several trees that he had
to go around or lift his machine over. He must have
worked hard at some of the obstructions. The tracks
showed that he lifted the bike pretty high and maneuvered around and through some rather intricate
places. He was determined, but finally he came to a
place where half a dozen trees had blown down in a
crisscross pattern across the road. He had tried to get
around the right side, then the left side. No way. He
gave up and went home. Nature was outlawing motor
vehicles from the forest long before the pressure
groups.

There was no sign that anyone else had hiked farther up the road all season. It had been weeks since it rained much but there were no footprints in the dirt, no broken stems, no disturbed stones or sticks. It was quiet but not silent. A faint breeze rustled the forest. Birds sang. In the distance a stream splashed on its rocks. It was like a symphony melting into the beauty of the forest.

We walked on. Meri stopped to pick some plants for her collection. She started that collection as a project for a biology class and kept at it long after the class was over. She loves the forests and mountains. And she has an insatiable curiosity about them. She's forever examining things and researching them. That plant collection led to a succession of years when I could expect to stop several times whenever we drove over a forest road because "there's a flower I don't have yet."

I sat on a downed tree and waited for her to catch up. The forest around me was a tangle of trees and brush. Flowers and grass mixed a pretty bouquet on the old road. The sky was blue and puffy clouds peeked between the trees. The air was warm. Around a curve in the road, high on a slope, I could glimpse part of an old clearcut. That, I suppose, is where the road leads. It was some miles more to the clearcut and we didn't get that far that day. But it seemed interesting. The trees had regrown man-high or more. It looked like there were still flowers and bushes between the trees. Berry bushes, probably. Must be a great place when the berries are ripe. If there's water there it would make a perfect place to camp. I intend to find out.

While I waited for Meri to catch up, I absorbed the beauty of that old road and I wondered about the letter I had received a few months earlier. The letter was from one of the big guns of the wilderness-

conservation movement, a famous name among the
establishment of famous names. I had met him a time
or two and enjoyed him. We had visited many of the
same backcountry places, and we shared an interest
in their history. I guess we talked for hours on end.
But there was no mistake. He was a wilderness-
conservationist. A crusader, I think, rather than a
profit seeker or pressure reliever, but a strong believ-
er nevertheless. Not open to opposing ideas.

He had sent the letter in response to an article I had
written for a magazine. The article was about the
same kind of thing this book is about and he took
strong exception to it. "Have you seen the 'lovely'
mess left up the White Chuck some years back?" he
asked. "The ruination of the valley was useful as a
conservationist propaganda tool. Was it worth ruin-
ing for our generation for the purpose? The trees are
gone now, and perhaps the termites have eroded
much of the lumber now in buildings."

I'm not sure why he sees a ruined valley where I see
exquisite beauty. I don't expect either of us will ever
learn to see with the other's eyes. And I don't think
there's any reason we should. The mountains have
something for everyone. And enough for everybody.
Certainly there's nothing wrong with setting aside,
freezing some of the mountain's lands into regimented, regulated land wilderness. Nothing wrong
with that. I enjoy it myself.

But that's not the only kind of beauty, adventure,
and wonder the mountains have to offer. It's wrong to
deny the other kinds. It's wrong to give the mountains exclusively to the people who demand that kind
of experience. And it's wrong for a few people to be
heard while everyone else is ignored.

Those few people can't keep shutting up the
people's land forever, despite their sophisticated propaganda and their slick politics. Sooner or later the

people will react, demand that the public land be open to everyone. If that demand is thwarted because the pressure groups have gained control of the decision making process, the stress will grow to explosive proportions. The result may well be that the entire wilderness system will be abolished, that when the people regain control they will be so angered and disgusted they will throw out the whole concept of wilderness-by-fiat. Environmental Protection Agency administrator Russell Train was right when he said there could be a backlash of public resentment.

It would be terrible if we lost all the land wilderness simply because the pressure groups tried to grab too much.

NOTES

CHAPTER ONE:

1. Earth Day has not been widely observed for several years. News
   media which once published vast amounts of material on the
   environment have turned to other subjects. In Washington a
   candidate for governor, a scientist herself, openly criticized the
   state's environmental laws and promised to use common sense in
   environmental matters. She was elected despite strong opposition by environmental groups. An environmental organization
   recently advertised for new members on the grounds that the
   organization was needed to revive legislative interest in the
   movement.
2. Down considerably from the 30,000 of the day before but still
   three times more than the 360 total that showed up at the bird
   clinic. The 1,000 figure, incidentally, referred to all birds, not just
   geese.
3. Douglas since has retired.
4. Kennecott would have to build a road of some sort up the valley to
   get its machinery to the mine and the ore to civilization. The
   wilderness conservationists held that the road would destroy the
   beauty of the entire valley, even those places where the road could
   not be seen. The mine, at this writing, has not been developed and
   I know of no efforts to develop it.
5. Many logging jobs are similar to mining tasks and loggers often
   are interchangeable with miners. Mostly what they want is physical work or work on machinery located in the mountains away
   from the big city.

CHAPTER THREE:

1. Vol. IV, no. 17, 50 cents.
2. The fair, in Spokane, was billed as an environmental fair but it failed to give over its decision—making processes to conservation leaders and they became decidedly cool. FOE had an exhibit but ridiculed the fair nevertheless.

CHAPTER FOUR:

1. Wilderness-conservation propagandists claim both Muir and Pinchot as pioneers in the wilderness cause. Not so. Pinchot devoted his career to the proposition that the people's land should benefit the people. There is some reason to believe Muir also saw reasonable limits to his proposals to lock up the land.
2. *Battle of the Wilderness*, New York, Praeger Publishers, 1974.
3. Frome, p. 91.
4. *Ibid.*, p. 84.
5. *Ibid.*, pp 98, 184, 78, 82, 83, 70.
6. The timing makes it obvious the editorial was based on Dr. Buckman's statement. But, just to be sure, I checked all my Forest Service sources. None knew of any such admission by any Forest Service spokesman. Certainly the service had not officially made any such decision. Nor did any Forest Service official I could find privately feel the use of DDT had been unnecessary. I talked to Dr. Buckman personally and he was quite upset to think the editorial was a result, even indirectly, of something he had said.

CHAPTER FIVE:

1. The park took a large portion of the national forest. The remains of that forest were consolidated with the Snoqualmie National Forest. Although the consolidated unit is called the Mount Baker-Snoqualmie National Forest, the Mount Baker, for all practical purposes, no longer exists.
2. Let it not be said I am opposed to the park. Parks are great. I'm for them and the North Cascades is a good place for one. But I believe strongly they should not be formed, even in part, to punish a public agency for refusing to accept the dictates of a pressure group.
3. Such as a reporter who wants to hike without regimentation or a logger who wants to work, or a poor person who wants lumber he can afford to build a house with.
4. That illustrates one of the major deceptions practiced by wilderness-conservation groups. They pretend that the land they want will be destroyed for certain uses if it is not classified for

their special designs. Not true. The land in question at that hearing could, with or without wilderness classification, be used by the gay liberationists. Even if it were clearcut, it still could be used for outdoor activities, including hiking.

5. For many of the pressure relievers among the pressure group membership, that is a reason they are involved. Even though they may not receive any publicity personally. Just being part of a movement that attracts attention feeds their ego enough to make the effort worthwhile.

6. The pressure groups catch more than just reporters in that trap. Recently Congressman Lloyd Meeds distributed to his constituents a questionnaire asking if they approved of a "timber industry" bill for the Alpine Lakes area of the Cascade Mountains. The bill had been written by a coalition of commercial interests and people who had no interest in the Alpine Lakes except recreation. The recreationists included campers, hikers, motor bikes and others, plus large numbers of horsemen. The wording on his questionnaire left them dismayed, hurt and angry. He apparently had rejected their desires out-of-hand as commercial and, therefore, opposed to the interests of the people.

7. It fits their propaganda, too. They love to publicize pictures of charming, innocent, pure, young animals and imply they will be "destroyed" if the pressure groups dictates are not obeyed.

CHAPTER SIX:

1. That supply is finite and we must also create better methods for reusing metals and we must stop using them for unessential purposes; but that is not to say we should not put the metal that remains in the ground at our disposal.

2. The Boy Scouts published in 1974 a Southwestern states "Wilderness Digest" of federal wilderness-use regulations and how to cope with them. It is 64 pages long.

3. That explains the wilderness conservationist's equivocation about the permits. The permits demonstrate that the groups have the power to force the service to require them but at the same time they demonstrate that the wilderness conservationists must report to the ranger station before they themselves can enter the wilderness.

4. Since then the Forest Service has conducted an anti-litter campaign that has resulted in a 90 percent reduction in the amount of litter found in the back country, proof, I believe, that people will respond to wilderness needs if they know what they are and why they are needed.

5. Biologists believe there are more deer in the Pacific Northwest now than when Lewis and Clark visited the region, because man's clearcut logging practices have provided more of their kind of

environment than was available originally.

6. I suspect it actually was bail but the ranger apparently didn't make that clear. Assuming, of course, that it wasn't simply an old-fashioned shake down.

CHAPTER SEVEN:

1. Frome, p. 146.
2. *Ibid.*, p. 147.
3. That is not to say, of course, that wilderness-conservationists should be ignored. Only that they should be considered in proportion to their numbers. Whatever ideas they submit should—must—be considered but as ideas not as dictation.
4. Loggers are leaving less and less of this "slash" material as the wood resource becomes more scarce and more valuable. It is becoming increasingly feasible to take every piece of wood they can, in some cases, leaves, bark, and all. The scene can be strikingly beautiful, either way.
5. Frome, pp. 181-3.

INDEX